PRAISE FOR *FROM*

From Self-Talk to Soul-Talk *bring͓ ͓͓͓͓͓ wisdom into our everyday lives with practical insights and simple tools to help us awaken to our true selves.*
—**Arianna Huffington, Founder and CEO, Thrive Global**

A masterpiece! Russell guides you to a deeper connection with yourself to unlock so much more potential than you knew you had. Delve into a self-reflective journey that will transform your life in every way. A must read!
—**Marshall Goldsmith, *New York Times* #1 best-selling author of *Triggers, Mojo,* and *What Got You Here Won't Get You There***

I have known Russell Bishop for more than forty years, and we have laughed, loved, partnered, argued, and learned from each other. I have personally experienced virtually everything Russell has said and suggested in this book and can validate them wholeheartedly as perspectives and exercises that have also served me on a similar lifelong path of self-awareness. Having spent countless hours observing his trainings, coaching, and consulting engagements, his insightfulness and incisiveness have no parallel.
—**David Allen, best-selling author of *Getting Things Done,* and CEO of David Allen Company**

From Self-Talk to Soul-Talk *is a master class in awakening, awareness, and acceptance that parallels TM in many ways—both are simple, natural, and effortless. Drawing upon a lifelong pursuit of timeless wisdom, Russell provides a practical guide for transcending the distractions of day-to-day life and receiving inner guidance from our souls.*
—**Bob Roth, CEO David Lynch Foundation and best-selling author of *Strength in Stillness***

At last, the book we've all been waiting for. Personally, I've been waiting some 40+ years, which is when I first met Russell and was introduced to the very unusual ideas and practices that I found in his experientially based Insight Seminars, and which are even more relevant today than they were when they were introduced. I want to be clear. What Russell shares in this book are nothing less than the very principles and practices that are assisting us all in changing life in a positive direction on this fragile planet today. Thank you, Russell, for bringing your practical wisdom forward at the perfect time for us all to benefit.
—**Ron Hulnick, President, University of Santa Monica and best-selling coauthor of *Loyalty to Your Soul***

"A Masterpiece!"
—**Jesus Garcia, D.S.S. and author of** *The Love of a Master*

Russell Bishop has downloaded decades of learning and sweating into a book for all seasons. Read it, pass it around, use its sage advice. Russell is a practicing sage, a rare person and now you can get his soul talk. Buy, Share, Enjoy.
—**John O'Neil, President of Center for Leadership Renewal and bestselling author of the** *Paradox of Success* **and** *Leadership Akido*

Russell Bishop has the gift of "hidden in plain sight" practical wisdom and like a fine wine he ripens with time which is why you need to read his latest revolutionary evolution, From Self-Talk to Soul-Talk.
—**Mark Goulston, MD, and author of** *Just Listen: Discover the Secret to Getting Through to Absolutely Anyone*

After working with tens of thousands of people, Russell Bishop finally shares the secret formula for how to live a successful life providing the instructions every being should be given upon their birth. It's the Bible of human growth and potential.
—**Heide Banks, psychotherapist and relationship expert**

From Self-Talk to Soul-Talk *is full of insight, combining spiritual ideas with practicality in a way that will enlighten many. Included throughout are questions that encourage self-reflection, allowing one's own answers and guidance to surface. Bishop adds additional exercises and resources in the appendix to further facilitate a pragmatic approach to living a spiritual life.*
—**Barbara B. Hebert, PhD, President, Theosophical Society in America**

From Self-Talk to Soul-Talk *is a masterful guidebook that eloquently shows us how to recognize, awaken, integrate, and embody the extraordinariness of our psychological and true spiritual self, amidst the ordinariness of our everyday lives. Filled with keen insights and potent exercises that are designed to connect us with our deepest heart's longings,* From Self-Talk to Soul-Talk *is a treasure and pleasure to read—a seminal work and must-read that clearly reveals the road we all must travel to embody our full potential.*
—**Richard Miller, PhD, Founder of iRest Institute and author of** *Yoga Nidra: The iRest Meditation Practice for Deep Relaxation and Healing* **and** *The iRest Program for Healing PTSD*

FROM SELF-TALK TO
SOUL-TALK

Becoming More of
Who You Truly Are

RUSSELL BISHOP

CONSCIOUSLIVING
PRESS

Copyright 2022 by Russell Bishop
All rights reserved. No part of this book may be used or reproduced in any manner whatsoever without written permission except in the case of brief quotations embodied in critical articles or reviews.

CONSCIOUSLIVING
PRESS

Published by Conscious Living Press

Paperback ISBN: 978-1-7379571-4-0
Ebook ISBN: 978-1-7379571-5-7

Printed in the United States of America
10 9 8 7 6 5 4 3 2 1

Produced by GMK Writing and Editing, Inc.
Managing Editor: Katie Benoit
Copyeditor: Josh Rosenberg
Proofread by EpsteinWords
Text design and composition by Libby Kingsbury
Cover design by Libby Kingsbury
Printed by IngramSpark
Visit the author at www.russellbishop.com
Write the author at russell@russellbishop.com

For Inez, my loving wife, incredible best friend, and partner on my way back home to God.

CONTENTS

ACKNOWLEDGMENT

JOHN-ROGER—The Teacher Appears
When the Student Is Ready

While many have encouraged me to write this book over the years, my good friend and spiritual teacher, John-Roger (J-R), has been an inspiration, and a constant supporter in the process. I first met John-Roger in 1973 through his writings and lectures on "Soul Transcendence."

At the time, I was a newly minted educational psychologist, with a background in Gestalt psychology, personal transformation, and large group awareness training. While the educational and psychological approaches to learning and development had served me well, enabling me to make great strides in self-confidence and self-expression, I still felt a bit disconnected in ways I did not understand.

Through the writings and practical study techniques J-R taught, I became aware that the disconnect was between my true self, with my soul, and the negative self-images I had adopted through a variety of life experiences and challenges. Although I had developed a pretty good intellectual ability, explored the depths of my emotions, and was in fine health, something still felt amiss.

The more I tested the techniques he suggested, the more I discovered a deeper connection into my true self. I found that the quality of my life experience improved dramatically, even if the circumstances seemed little different to those on the outside looking in. Paradoxically, the deeper I became aware of myself as soul, the more I could create in terms of material-level abundance and the less it seemed to matter. As I discovered the real source of satisfaction, I found my life improving in amazing and inspiring ways.

AUTHOR'S NOTE

My Journey into Awakening—Why I Wrote This Book

*The two most important days of your life are the day you were
born and the day you find out why.*

—Mark Twain

This book offers insights, lessons, and perspectives I have found
useful in my path of becoming more aware, in letting my true self,
my soul, take the lead. My good friend and spiritual mentor, John-
Roger, began encouraging me to write a book about my experiences
and life lessons over 30 years ago. Apparently, I needed a lot of support and encouragement to finally sit down and do the writing.

The information, frameworks, and exercises which follow have
proven useful to me in my own journey. Not everything will resonate with you, so please take what works and leave the rest behind.
There's nothing to believe here—just perspectives to try on, to experiment with, and discover what may have meaningful value to you.

You will undoubtedly recognize many of these lessons and suggestions. They comprise what many call ancient wisdoms. Indeed,
I heard most of these many times before I began applying them in
any kind of consistent manner. My experience continues to show
me that there's a great difference between "knowing about" these
wisdoms and actually implementing them.

No matter how good I think I may have become with these practices, I find they require constant attention and conscious application on my part. I have been reminded countless times that *we teach that which we most need to learn.* Far from a "one and done" kind of curriculum, these are more akin to "use it or lose it."

A couple of notes about my style as a writer: I tend to write as though I'm speaking with you. As a result, I keep slipping back and forth between I, we, you, and us. My English teachers must be shaking their heads in despair. However, this mixed-use of pronouns is purposeful because I am a student of this information as well as a teacher of it and, while both student and teacher, I am also a co-worker right along with everyone else.

I also tend to repeat myself from time to time, bringing some examples, stories, metaphors, and other references back several times, each in slightly different contexts. Why? Simply because some of these insights will land differently depending on the situation or application. In my own path of awakening, I find that I often need to hear something a few times—well, multiple times actually—before I begin to discover the deeper implications.

The rest of this section is more of a mini-autobiography, providing an overview of key moments in my early life that opened the door to my deeper awakening.

I invite you to come on your version of this journey, and as you do, let your inner wisdom guide you on your path.

My Journey into Awakening

From the time I can remember thinking about why my life mattered, I have been on a quest to learn, to discover, to become ever more aware.

I grew up in a Presbyterian family—two uncles were ministers, my dad was an elder in the church, and I attended services every week. I never felt particularly inspired by the services themselves, much less the sermons; however, I did experience considerable expansion, peace, even grace in the music.

While I was attracted to something that I would later call mystical or spiritual, I was simultaneously repelled by the apparent disconnect between words and behaviors. Some part of me noticed the disconnect and yet compelled me to return week after week.

To be clear, I could not have articulated the disconnect that I was experiencing, much less that a lifelong search was upon me. However, the inner experience was not just undeniable, but also palpable.

The church had a youth program for teens which met on Wednesdays. I found Gary, the youth minister, to be "different," more attuned in some way to that ineffable quality of experience that attracted me. I didn't know what I was experiencing, but I did know that it seemed important, so I began paying attention.

When I was about 16 years old, these weekly youth meetings began focusing on life purpose and meaning. It was then that I first began to ask myself what I wanted out of life. And why. Somehow, I was dimly aware that my question might be poorly formed, because what I really wanted could not be measured in terms of external, material things.

I was beginning to ask, explore, and become aware of my true self, something I later learned was my soul. But at 16, this budding awareness was embryonic at best.

What I wanted had much more to do with how I experienced life. I was becoming increasingly aware that my internal experience and response to life had much more value and meaning than any tangible or worldly thing.

You Can Never Get Enough of What You Don't Really Want

At about that same time, a marvelous and quirky high school teacher of mine, Mr. Siringer, introduced our class to the world of poetry and philosophy. On one of our frequent visits to the City Lights bookstore in San Francisco, he introduced us to the works of Eric Hoffer, a local longshoreman, poet, and philosopher.

Something Mr. Hoffer wrote struck me in a profound yet subtle way, something that has stayed with me ever since, something that has served as a unique kind of North Star. He wrote, "you can never get enough of what you don't really need to make you happy." I have since paraphrased this profound awareness: you can never get enough of what you don't really want.

What is it that I really want? My self-talk can go on and on about anything from chocolate to money to jobs to houses to . . . I was coming to learn that no amount of any of these provides lasting satisfaction. Short-term happiness? Sure. Deeper satisfaction? Not so much.

The (Not So) Gentle Awakening

A few years later, I found myself in my first encounter group while a sophomore at the University of California, Davis. I had no idea what an encounter group was or that I was attending one. (Encounter groups were popular forms of small-group personal growth work where participants experienced various forms of interaction, feedback, problem solving, and role play to gain insights into themselves, others, and the group itself.) The meeting was billed as team building for members of the newly elected student council.

My father had passed away that summer from leukemia and I was feeling insecure, fragile, and basically lost. Much like the proverbial fish-out-of-water, I found myself in unfamiliar territory, with a fragile arrogance surrounding an intense insecurity. My self-talk assured me that there were two effective strategies for staying safe: withdraw or criticize. There are times, to this day, when I struggle with that pattern.

Adopting my preferred strategy of "hiding," I opted for the sidelines as this group of would-be-future-legislators were probed about our intentions, dreams, fears, and hopes. I soon learned there is nothing so futile as trying to hide as I became the focus of our facilitators and my fellow student legislators.

The more I was asked questions, the more I deflected the spotlight by turning those questions into statements, questions, or criticisms about others. In my desperate attempts to deflect any focus on my never-ending supply of insecurity, I unintentionally, but extremely successfully, exposed myself and became even more vulnerable.

As other student council members were invited to comment on what I had to say, the feedback directed my way was less than gentle (bordering on brutal) but clearly accurate. Everything I was trying to hide was becoming quite visible.

The experience was painful—my impenetrable shell had been pierced. Shattered. Fortunately, the encounter group was facilitated by two amazingly caring and gifted leaders, Ernie Gourdine and Van Richards. Devastated, embarrassed, and strangely relieved at the same time, I soon found myself crying in Ernie's arms.

As that fragile shell cracked, my true self began to emerge. The experience helped me realize that the emptiness I felt inside came from the barriers I had placed there to protect myself. I had imprisoned myself within my own defenses.

My self-talk tried keeping people away to avoid even more hurt and pain and instead wound up entrapped in that very hurt and pain. As it turned out, the ever-present hurt and pain was, in fact, self-inflicted isolation. I worked hard to keep people away because "they" must be the ones hurting me. And all the while it was "me" doing all the inflicting rather than "them."

Beneath the hurt and pain, I started to get a glimmer of the "true self" I had begun seeking a few years earlier. My soul-talk was quietly pointing me to the deeper aspects of who I truly am, rather than the "defective" person my self-talk assured me I must be. I began to discover that any connection with my true self, my soul, was more valuable than anything I had ever sought or experienced.

The Rude Awakening

If you wanted to put the world to rights,
who should you begin with: yourself or others?

—ALEKSANDR SOLZHENITSYN

In 1971, I found myself on a strike line at UC Berkeley, just outside Sather Gate. "On strike, shut it down. All power to all people." That was our mantra. On this spring day, Sheriff Madigan, and the Blue Meanies as we called his officers, instigated the daily riot as they plowed through our protest line randomly striking protesters with their batons. Shortly thereafter I was hit by a tear gas canister.

As instructed, I picked up the canister to throw it back. No one warned me how hot it would be. Perhaps it was shock, perhaps it was divine guidance, perhaps one led to the other, but suddenly I was outside my body, looking back at myself. Now, I know this may sound beyond weird, but somehow, I was about 20 feet away and up another 20 feet, looking back at an angry young man, bearded with long hair screaming, "Why don't you a**holes love us."

And, BAM, I was back in my body with a profound awareness flooding over me: My message was peace, love, and caring, while my strategy was to yell, scream, and throw things.

Disconnect, disconnect, disconnect!

I was stunned by the suddenly apparent conflict between my actions and my true motives—fighting for peace yet screaming to be loved could not be more oxymoronic, and yet until that moment, I had not come close to noticing. Although this entire experience lasted but a few seconds, the impact has been lifelong.

I dropped the tear gas canister, left the strike line, and never returned. An hour later, I found myself at a friend's apartment on Shattuck Avenue where I shaved my beard, cut my hair, and stared into the mirror for a good hour, asking myself, "who are you" as tears streamed down my face.

This experience shocked me onto a path of searching for a way to live a more conscious life, characterized by loving, caring, and compassion. My self-talk had been pushing me into "action," which turned out to be just another form of criticism, anger, and avoidance.

That tear gas canister somehow enabled me to hear my soul-talk with a whole new level of clarity as I stared into that mirror asking myself, "who are you?": *Russell, you are here to take action toward what you prefer rather than point out the error of other people and their ways. You cannot fight for peace, loving, or caring. You must BE loving, caring, and full of peace.*

How's that for guidance?

My soul-talk did not tell me what to do much less how to do it. It pointed me in the direction of the experience I truly wanted. As Mr. Hoffer might have said, no amount of anger, accusations, or tear gas would fulfill me. I didn't want angry confrontation about the wrongs of the world. What I wanted was a greater experience of peace, loving, and caring—for me, for others, for the world.

Clearly, my soul-talk was encouraging me to build a solid inner foundation from which to act. It took a scorching hot tear gas canister to awaken me to reality. I could not bring peace to myself, much less the world if I harbored anger, resentment, and outrage inside.

It took another two years before I met my spiritual teacher, John-Roger. J-R, as we called him, helped me understand the difference between my "self" (with a little "s") and my true Self (with a capital "S"). That true self is the soul.

Both have voices, one louder than the other, one deeper and more meaningful. The deeper, more meaningful voice is also the softer voice.

INTRODUCTION

Which Voice Am I Listening To?

There is a voice that doesn't use words. Listen.

—Rumi

We all have a louder inner voice telling us what's important, what matters, and what we should want. Sometimes, that louder voice, what I call our self-talk, provides some useful direction and advice. Other times, not so much. The limiting side of my self-talk shows up when some part of me criticizes what I am doing, reminding me that life is hard, or that a "good idea" will never work. My self-talk may also latch onto an idea it heard somewhere else and keep harping on me to pursue someone else's dream.

We also have a much softer inner voice, quietly encouraging us to look more deeply, to look past the glitter and glamour of life's temporal distractions and discover that which is truly lasting. I call this softer voice my soul-talk. It emanates from the deepest part of my true self, from my soul.

In my experience, *Becoming More of Who You Truly Are* requires learning to listen to that deeper voice, proactively consulting with my true self for advice and counsel about the choices and options in front of me. The more practiced I have become at listening to that softer voice, the more penetrating it becomes, almost as though it were the louder voice. The more I have paid attention, the more it has helped with my personal life (my family, health, and well-being), as well as with my business and professional life.

Dr. Shad Helmstetter coined the term *self-talk* in his wildly popular 1986 self-help book, *What to Say When You Talk to Your Self.* Dr. Helmstetter specified that most of us have an inner critic that is all too happy to point out our flaws and foibles. He counseled his readers to reframe the negative dialogue (inner diatribe in my case) into a more positive, expansive, and uplifting set of affirmations, a new form of positive self-talk. (An affirmation is a positive, present-tense statement about a change or difference I would prefer to experience. For example, *I am a loving, caring, and worthwhile man* is more useful in supporting a desired change than incessant self-talk criticism about always coming up short, always being rejected, or never being enough. More on affirmations in Chapter 9.)

Dr. Helmstetter's book helped me quite a bit as I learned about affirmations and how to reframe negative self-talk into something more constructive. By combining this work with the wisdom of the true self or soul that I was learning in my spiritual studies with John-Roger, I began to notice the distinction between two inner voices.

My self-talk tends to be loud, dominating, and relentless. I have learned that pausing the negative self-talk and listening more closely to that softer, wiser soul-talk can produce amazing insights, guidance, and inner support.

Do You Have an Obnoxious Roommate Living in Your Head?

Arianna Huffington often refers to that critical self-talk as the "obnoxious roommate living in our head." In an article published in her *Thrive Global* online magazine she wrote:

> *Even our worst enemies don't talk about us the way we talk to ourselves. I call this voice the obnoxious roommate living in our head. It feeds on putting us down and strengthening our insecurities and doubts. I wish someone would invent a tape*

recorder that we could attach to our brains to record every-thing we tell ourselves. We would realize how important it is to stop this negative self-talk. It means pushing back against our obnoxious roommate with a dose of wisdom . . . I have spent many years trying to evict my obnoxious roommate and have now managed to relegate her to only occasional guest appearances in my head.

What would it be like if those guest appearances were much fewer?

When things go south in life, my self-talk will insist that it's "their" fault, that nothing will ever improve, etc., ad nauseum. Even more debilitating, my self-talk would have me believe that underneath it all, I'm defective, incapable, and hopelessly stuck.

Fortunately, my soul-talk is there throughout the negativity, constantly there to support me in greater wisdom, loving, and upliftment. Even while my self-talk points to the impossibility of it all, to the "I can't because" stories I learned as a kid, my soul-talk quietly encourages me to discover new possibilities.

You have probably heard some version of, "Let those who have ears, hear." We all have the ears to hear the soul-talk; they're just not our physical ears, but our "inner ears." Learning to listen inwardly can make a huge difference.

While I will suggest that your soul-talk is the more useful voice, your self-talk will not be blamed or criticized. It's only trying to do what it deems best for you. What if your self-talk could partner with your true self, with your soul-talk, to make things even better?

What Do I Mean by the Soul?

When you examine the lives of the most influential people who have ever walked among us, you discover one thread that winds through them all. They have been aligned first with their spiritual nature and only then with their physical selves.

—ALBERT EINSTEIN

We are not human beings having a spiritual experience.
We are spiritual beings having a human experience.

—PIERRE TEILHARD DE CHARDIN

Given that I'm writing about something I'm calling "soul-talk," I ought to provide a context, definition, or explanation of soul. Matters spiritual can be fraught with all kinds of implied moral imperatives, dogmas, instructions, and rituals. Sometimes they come with hard and fast boundaries of "right and wrong."

I am not writing to provide dogma or right-wrong moral imperatives. You don't need any particular spiritual or religious perspective to gain value from this book.

Many people are turned off by anything suggesting religion or religious practices, often due to past experiences with restrictive dogmas or practices preached or required. Even if you have been through and rebelled against some form of restrictive practice, you should find some sound, actionable suggestions here absent of restriction— no dogma, nothing to believe, just ideas to test and discover if they work for you. Keys such as Awareness and Choice work regardless of your view of religion, spirit, or the divine.

Be assured that I am not out to convert you to any kind of religious or spiritual point of view. I figure that's between you, and, well, *you* to determine. My spiritual point of view can be summed up rather simply:

- God never named itself, including the name "God"—it took human beings to come up with the various names we use.

- All things come from God, Source, the Divine, Spirit, or any other name you might prefer.

- God loves all of Its creation.

- Not one Soul will be lost.

When I refer to Spirit, the Divine, or soul, these are the basic tenets underlying what I have to share with you. There's plenty here to disagree with depending on your point of view—I'm just sharing mine so you know where I'm coming from.

Religion and the Myth of the Spiritual Path

Many traditions teach that the spiritual path is an inward one, and yet many seek spiritual awareness as though it lies somewhere outside of themselves.

It may be worth noting that the word *religion* comes from the Latin word *legare* which simply means to connect; the prefix, "re," means again. So, rather than meaning anything about a defined or dogmatic set of practices, a religious experience may well be one that "reconnects" me with something that I was previously connected to.

If we are reconnecting to something we were previously connected to, then the path may be as simple as turning inward. While the spiritual path metaphor is an attractive one in that it suggests there is work still to do, steps to take, in order to arrive at your destination, it also can be seen as an illusion or distraction.

I sometimes refer to this as *The Myth of the Spiritual Path*. Being on a path suggests a beginning, an end, and some distance to go before I arrive at my destination, a gap between where I am now and where I need to be in the future. Many philosophers and traditions have suggested that the notion of a spiritual path is an illusion, teaching that the spiritual path is an inward one.

Various versions of "being on the path" suggest that what we seek is already present—God, spirit, soul, or whatever other language you prefer is already here, right now, patiently waiting for us to notice. Francis of Assisi suggested this in the 12th century and Rumi echoed that sentiment in the 13th century, writing, "what you seek is seeking you."

The Bible counsels that "the kingdom of heaven is within." Tolstoy wrote an entire book entitled *The Kingdom of God Is Within*

You. In his novel, *Siddhartha,* Hermann Hesse wrote, "What could I say to you that would be of value, except that perhaps you seek too much, that as a result of your seeking you cannot find."

I once heard a yogi master answer a question from one of his devotees who was struggling with finding enlightenment, "Perhaps you should stop seeking and start finding."

If the spiritual path leads to spirit or enlightenment, to *Becoming More of Who You Truly Are,* to being in the heart of God—feel free to substitute any language that works well for you here—then where do you have to go in order to arrive? Better yet, where do you have to start? Perhaps the starting place and the destination are the same.

Do You Have a Master Teacher?

Another way to think about your soul-talk is to imagine that you have your own inner master, teacher, or guide quietly illuminating "the path" inward. Some find it helpful to imagine their inner master as a representative of a higher source with which they already have some familiarity.

I have met people who consider that Jesus is alive in their hearts, guiding them back home. Others relate to an inner Buddha, while others imagine a more cosmic form without necessarily assigning a specific figure to the inner master. Still others find that different forms appear at different times covering a range from Jesus to Buddha, from Mohammed to Zarathustra, and angels of all manner.

I don't think it matters which form you most resonate with. The Divine can and will take any form that is useful to you. After all, as I noted earlier, "It" never named Itself.

WHAT IF?

Throughout this book, I will refer to what I call the "What If" principle. "What if" simply means, *what if* something you read here is true? If something is true, it doesn't matter whether our self-talk believes it or likes it—it's just true, regardless of who said it! If you can suspend self-talk judgment and just play "as if" these ideas might be true, you will have the opportunity to test them in the laboratory of your own life.

If you examine an idea with an open mind, and the idea works for you, then you have added one more element of "truth" to your toolset which might help you create life as you would prefer. If you experiment with one of these ideas and find that it doesn't work for you, then just leave it behind. If, however, you reject an idea out of hand for any number of self-talk reasons (never heard that before, couldn't be true, etc.), and it happens to be true, you may wind up settling for less than your preferred life simply because your self-talk wouldn't let you experiment with it.

The important thing isn't whether you agree or disagree with anything I will write here—what's important is whether you can use any of it to improve the quality of your life experience in ways that are meaningful to you.

CHAPTER 1

AWAKENING

The one you are looking for is the one who is looking.

—Francis of Assisi

To delve further into the power and distinctions between self-talk and soul-talk, we first need to explore two of the most critical aspects of improving our experience of life—awakening and awareness. Both are so natural that each is easily overlooked or misunderstood.

These two keys are much like the old saw of which comes first, the chicken or the egg. Sometimes, it takes a dose of awareness to awaken, and other times it requires awakening to become aware. Since awakening comes before awareness alphabetically speaking, let's start there.

Many spiritual paths actively use the notion of awakening to describe the purpose of the spiritual journey. However, rarely does anyone take the time to deconstruct the term *awaken.*

An awakening takes place when something that was previously asleep comes back into conscious awareness *again.* Notice the emphasis on *again.* Something that awakens was previously asleep—that part is probably obvious. Equally obvious and rarely considered is that *something asleep was previously awake.*

If the goal of the spiritual journey is to awaken, then the spiritual path doesn't take us somewhere we are not as much as it awakens us to where we already are. In my lexicon, Spirit is present with and within me, but I may not be present with Spirit from time to time. Indeed, I find that I often fall asleep to Spirit in my daily life.

In this sense of awakening, you may find that experimenting with these keys or suggestions will help you come into a more profound awareness and alignment with who you are deep inside your being. For some, that will mean reconnecting with a spiritual source, with the Divine, with God. For others, it may mean connecting with a deeper sense of who you are, something beyond personality and the mind. It is the deeper connection that matters most, irrespective of what we may call it.

Merriam-Webster tells us that to awaken, means to:

- "cease sleeping"
- "become aroused or active again"
- "become conscious or aware of something."

Perhaps the most significant aspect of awakening is found in the words *active again* which stand out in the middle of the three definitions. "Again" means it was active before.

In this sense, awakening is both a natural process as well as a great metaphor. If we move past the simplistic side of the physical body sleeping or awakening, we can move to something more profound, the awakening of consciousness.

There is an amazing depth of power in this notion of becoming "active again." You may recall from *The Myth of the Spiritual Path* in the Introduction, the word *religion* stems from the Latin *legare*, meaning to connect, with the prefix, "re," meaning again. So here we have a parallel meaning—to awaken again may well be the same as to connect again.

Awakening to Who You Already Are

When I created Insight Seminars in 1978 with John-Roger, we called the first seminar "The Awakening Heart" with a tag line of *Becoming*

More of Who You Truly Are. We chose the phrase "Awakening Heart" rather than referring to the mind, body, or emotions because the heart is the center of loving. In some spiritual traditions, the heart is considered the seat of the soul. Part of our reasoning was that as the heart awakens, we can become aware of a deeper level of knowledge or wisdom than the mind can perceive let alone understand. We called that "natural knowing."

Our premise was that we already possess this deeper wisdom; it just may be difficult to access given the brashness of our self-talk. Learning to listen and heed the more subtle messages from our soul-talk are important keys to creating the life we truly want, rather than the one our self-talk may be incessantly focusing on or settling for.

Have you ever heard someone say something like, "I just knew it in my heart"? Sometimes the heart "knows" something that the mind can't explain, and yet that natural knowing is there independent of what the mind or intellect can explain.

If you're a biblical scholar, you know Proverbs 23:7. One paraphrase reads, "As a man thinketh in his heart, so he becomes." Of course, this is not limited to men but applies to all of humankind. The key lies in the relationship between what we may be thinking in our hearts and what we become.

For some, this whole question of *thinking in your heart* is a bridge too far. How can you think in your heart? Well beyond some simplistic or idealistic notion, we now have neuroscience to provide evidence of something that Proverbs points toward.

In 1991, J. Andrew Armour MD, PhD, published an article citing the discovery of neurons in the heart, what he later called the "little brain in the heart." Neurons are the basic working unit of the brain, specialized cells that transmit information to other nerve cells, muscle, or gland cells. When neurons release brain chemicals, known as neurotransmitters, the electrical signals propagate like a wave to thousands of neurons, which in turn leads to thought formation. Armour discovered that the little brain in the heart sends more information to the mind-brain than vice versa. Subsequent studies have found multiple implications including the possibility that the "heart-brain" can even regulate pain (https://pubmed.ncbi.nlm.nih.gov/31728781/).

We also know that there are bundles of neurons in the gut which are directly connected to the brain. So, when someone says, "my gut tells me," there's something very real going on, perhaps a parallel to "I knew it in my heart." Sometimes we "just know" and there's little to be done or explained other than acknowledging that, well, sometimes we "just know." (If you want to read more on this, you might consider researching the gut and brain connection.)

For our purposes, we're going to work from the premise that this kind of knowing is both normal and natural. If this strains your imagination, for now, I'll ask you to play along with the "what if" game—*what if there is a source of intelligence naturally residing within us simply waiting for us to awaken to it, something beyond the brain or mind?* If that's true, wouldn't it be worth considering the possibility?

Sleeping Is OK Too

In the world of personal transformation, people often use the term *wake up*, sometimes as a gentle encouragement and more often as a pejorative—WAKE UP!—as though there were something wrong with the person who is "asleep."

While awakening can be a powerful process for becoming more of who we truly are, so too is sleeping after having been awake for a while. Sometimes, we need sleep to process what took place while we were awake.

In the early days of Insight, I was facilitating a seminar with John-Roger, and I was becoming increasingly irritated with someone I judged for being slow to awaken. John-Roger provided my own wake-up call by reminding me that sleep is part of the natural process of growth and awareness. He posed his example in the form of a question to me: "Would you wake up the sleeping baby so it can grow and learn faster?"

Growth, even awareness, can take place or develop while sleeping. I know I have had the experience of going to sleep in a state of confusion or consternation only to awaken in the morning with newfound clarity. Have you? If so, where did that come from?

One way of looking at this is to consider that in sleep, the mind (self-talk) is disengaged, allowing your true self, your soul-talk, to take the lead.

What Are You Awakening Toward?

Yesterday I was clever, so I wanted to change the world.
Today I am wise, so I am changing myself.

—RUMI

If you find yourself conflicted between what you think you want and what seems to really matter, perhaps the answer can be found in further awakening.

Surely you have experienced the temporary fulfillment that comes with giving into immediate pleasure-seeking behaviors ranging from eating all the ice cream to, well, you can fill in the blanks. We may be satisfied for a moment, but that soon passes. Even worse is the realization that we may have done a little bit of harm to our body or to our moral character along the way.

On the flip side, putting off fulfillment or meaningful engagement today in favor of an equally mirage-like illusion of a better future can lead us to wonder why we ever wanted that object of our focus in the first place, lamenting what we may have lost along the way. Have you been there? I know I have.

In both my personal life as well as my work with others, I have discovered the best answers often seem to come from within. Truly useful answers require that we awaken to who we already are, learning to listen to the quiet wisdom and guidance of our soul-talk.

The challenge with this lies in moving from the initial realization or "aha" moment of awakening into the messy and not-so-easy process of translating that awareness into something we can integrate consistently in daily life.

How to Awaken to What You Truly Want Out of Life

You might consider asking yourself two basic questions about awakening: *what are you awakening from* and *what are you awakening toward?*

I have learned a simple set of questions that have helped me become increasingly aware of my awakening process and discover more supportive choices both in the short term and the long term. The questions are implied in that provocative statement from Eric Hoffer I have previously paraphrased this way: *You can never get enough of what you don't really want.*

The implied questions, then, go something like this:

- What do you want?
- What experience are you hoping to find?
- What difference would that make to you?
- Why does that matter to you?
- What do you want?

For these questions to produce real meaning, you may have to cycle through them over and over a few times to allow deeper levels of awareness to filter up. Your self-talk will probably take over right from the start filling in answers ranging from the mundane (sex, money, travel, more or better fill-in-the-blank) to the stereotypical (house, job, kids). However, keep cycling these questions to yourself, asking more deeply each time "and why would that matter to me?"

You can ask these questions as a mental process, or perhaps more powerfully as a focus for your next meditation. You might also consider keeping a journal or notebook as you read this book, writing answers to the questions as well as tracking any insights that arise. Reviewing notes, answers, and insights over time can lead to ever-increasing awareness, discovering connections not previously perceived. Again, nothing to believe here—just something to try in the spirit of "What if?"

Questions like the ones above can be powerful tools for awakening to our deeper source of knowledge, to our true self. In my work, I rely heavily on questions for the simple reason that your own answers can be so much more meaningful and revelatory than any answers provided by me or someone else. If you were to answer a question with something like, "well, I don't know," I would typically ask this apparently cheeky question, "well, if you did know, what would the answer be?" Although this may appear facetious, the question points back to your inner knowing, to your soul-talk. It may take some practice, but if you will challenge yourself with something akin to "well, if I did know . . ." you may be surprised about the answers you will discover. And, most importantly, they will be your answers, not something foisted upon you by someone else.

MEDITATION EXERCISE

Accessing Your Soul-Talk

If meditation is new to you, this form should be easy to work with. If you already have a meditation practice, you may find this can be added to your current practice or simply tried as a new or different form. Feel free to experiment and find a simple way that works for you.

This meditation is designed to help you contact and communicate with aspects of your true self, with your soul-talk. Focusing on your breath can help you prepare for listening more deeply to your true self.

We will begin with a breathing technique known as box, square, or 4x4 breathing. From there we will suggest that you focus inwardly and invite your true self to come forward. We will then review the questions and answers from the section above on what you truly want. The idea is to engage in a bit of dialogue with your true self or soul-talk.

Once you are finished with the meditation, you can repeat the box breathing technique and return to your more conscious, aware state.

Box breathing is a simple technique that a person can do anywhere, including at a work desk or in a café. Also known as square or 4x4 breathing, this technique is taught in all manner of environments from MDs specializing in stress management to Navy SEALs and yoga studios. It can help you shift your energy and connect more deeply with your body, decreasing stress and introducing a state of calm or restfulness. You can use this technique just about any time, anywhere.

Before starting, sit with your back supported in a comfortable chair and your feet on the floor.

Box Breathing

1. Close your eyes and breathe in through your nose while counting to four slowly. Notice the air entering your lungs.

2. Now gently hold your breath inside while counting slowly to four. Try not to clamp your mouth or nose shut. Simply avoid inhaling or exhaling for another count of four.

3. Next, slowly and gently exhale for another count of four.

4. At the bottom of the fourth count, pause and hold for a count of four.

5. Repeat steps one to four at least three times. Ideally, repeat them for four minutes, or until you feel deeply relaxed or calm.

Invite your true self to come forward (feel free to substitute your inner master, teacher, guide, or, if you prefer, your soul).

- Some find it helpful to imagine they are in a peaceful place in nature, undisturbed by the day-to-day world. Others prefer to focus on their heart. There's no wrong way to do this, so just let yourself find your own relaxing, safe space and follow your own rhythm.

- Remaining in this quiet state, consciously invite that quieter part of you, your true self, to come forward as though it were sitting or standing in front of you. At first, you may not notice much difference, at least not in your body, mind, or emotions. You may simply feel more peaceful. Some will notice a presence, and some will even "see" a more defined form, perhaps even an image of yourself.

- As you begin to get a sense of this inward presence, tell it what you have been thinking about or considering, literally "speaking" to it as though it were physically in the room with you right now. You might want to start with an area of your life that needs attention or some choice you are considering. Let your true self know what you have been thinking, perhaps some limiting, critical aspect of your self-talk. Ask your true self or soul-talk what it would prefer that you notice or focus upon. Or you might want to ask your true self for its recommendations about a different choice you could consider making about where you are in your life right now.

- Feel free to make this more like a conversation with a trusted friend—pretty much a free-form exchange. Your soul-talk may have questions for you, ideas to consider, or suggestions for new options. Your true self may be direct with its advice or preferences, but rarely will the tone be harsh; rather, it most likely will be loving, supporting, and nurturing.

- If you hear something that you don't quite understand, ask for clarification.

- Be sure to repeat what you are hearing and how you imagine it can be implemented. Then ask if you heard correctly.

- Once you and your true self feel complete, thank your true self for its support and guidance, and return to your breathing process.

- When you are ready, slowly allow your eyes to open and focus back into the room where you find yourself.

- Write down what you heard. What did you learn? What insights did you gain?

As you reflect on these questions, sooner or later you may begin to hear the soft voice of your soul-talk speaking from deep within. If this kind of process is new to you, it may take a few sessions before the inner dialogue becomes clear. You may find your soul-talk focusing more on the qualitative experiences of life that produce deeper levels of fulfillment than the temporary nature of the material world.

With additional clarity on the qualitative experiences that you truly seek in life, two important questions follow: how to produce these qualitative experiences and how to produce them while going through the day-to-day reality of life in the world? If you find yourself struggling with these last two questions, you may once again be stuck in the dilemma of your self-talk speaking more loudly than your soul-talk. However, even if that's the case, you can still ask your soul-talk to keep speaking and do your best to listen more intently.

If you do so, you may be pleasantly surprised by how much more fulfillment you will discover in your daily life. The choice is yours— you can keep listening to the self-talk cautioning you against pursuing what matters most, or you can heed your soul-talk reminding you to focus on those deeper, qualitative experiences you truly seek.

CHAPTER 2

AWARENESS

*What is necessary to change a person
is to change his awareness of himself.*

—Abraham Maslow

Awareness may well be one of the most important life lessons we can learn. And learn. And learn. Absent of awareness, the existence of any of these lessons, let alone the value of their application, remains hidden to us. Awareness is an ongoing, everyday process rather than, "now that I'm aware of that, what's next?" Did you ever burn your hand on a hot stove and burn it again later? Clearly, a single instance of awareness may not be enough!

Once I become aware of something, what comes next is repeated application until it becomes second nature. Much like acquiring any new skill, considerable practice is required learning to apply the skill skillfully. You have probably "mastered" the awareness of the stove and yet may get the occasional reminder to "pay attention" when you get around hot things.

Lack of awareness can be as simple as driving down the road engaged in thought or conversation and driving right past your exit. Or putting your keys down somewhere and then struggling to find them.

Someone was "home" or "awake" enough to steer, brake, etc., and yet another part was somewhere else at the same time, kind of like sleepwalking (sleep-driving) through life. Said differently, we can have just enough awareness focused on the act of driving to keep the car on the road, but insufficient awareness to take the correct exit.

How does that work?

One way of looking at this is to recognize that you can move your awareness around. You can focus on your body, your mind, or your emotions; you can focus on what's right in front of you, dwell on the past, or dream about the future. In fact, you can be aware of several things at the same time.

If we direct our awareness to something other than what's right in front of us, we will likely miss something of importance, meaning, or substance, including choices that will help us get where we are going (like taking the right exit). When that happens to me, my self-talk often gives me a good dose of self-criticism—"you idiot." "Pay attention!" "Wake up!" "You're always screwing up." And all manner of "helpful" commentary.

Levels of Awareness

There are several levels of awareness that we can develop; in fact, you probably already have experience with most of these. Those levels are:

1. Physical: what's happening with your body, including physical sensations

2. Imaginative: what's happening in your imagination (fantasizing, daydreaming)

3. Emotional: what you are feeling emotionally

4. Mental: what you are thinking about (this one is a bit different from the imaginative level, characterized by more of an analytical type of thinking)

5. Unconscious: what's going on "behind the scenes"—influences for which you may not yet have developed awareness, but are there nonetheless

6. Spiritual or Soul-Centered: what's happening in your higher consciousness, in the source of who you truly are, your true self.

Much like driving the car, the challenge lies in becoming aware of multiple levels simultaneously without becoming distracted or too narrowly focused in the process.

Simple Awareness Can Often Be Curative

A major key in my awakening took place in 1969 when I read Fritz Perls's *Gestalt Therapy Verbatim.* One of his major concepts jumped out at me: *simple awareness can be curative.*

Perls was a trained psychoanalyst who pioneered a form of therapy focused on the present rather than analyzing the past. He often spoke about the role of awareness in helping people overcome various issues or neuroses, and generally improving their experience of life by discovering new choices.

Perls called the process of choosing, "response-ability." His work popularized the reframing of responsible and responsibility as *response-able* and *response-ability.* In any situation, we have multiple responses, options, or choices available coupled with different skill or ability levels to exercise those responses.

I later heard one of his colleagues at Esalen Institute paraphrasing Perls as having said that he stopped doing traditional psychoanalysis "because after years of analysis, most of my patients had well analyzed problems." He found that with increased awareness, his patients could discover new abilities to respond to previously challenging situations rather than remaining stuck in their current predicament, reinforced by reasons (analysis) from the past.

As his patients became aware of choices they were making along with the consequences of those choices, the patient could then find new ways to move past pain and suffering and toward a preferred life experience. Therefore, *simple awareness can be curative.*

When I first encountered this bit of wisdom and insight, I was knocked over by the simple elegance it conveys. If I am in pain, and if I am the one doing something that creates the pain, then maybe all I need to do is become aware of what I am doing to create the pain and make a different choice for the pain to go away. That assumes, of course, that I'm not particularly fond of pain.

Invariably, the source of my pain comes down to some choice I have made or some choice I have refused to acknowledge or make, even down to the choice not to choose. The lack of awareness leads to pain or suffering of one kind or another and the illusion of being stuck.

The impact of Fritz Perls's insight that *simple awareness can be curative* continues to influence my life to this day some 50 years later—without awareness, choices seem to be in short supply. As I become increasingly aware, I discover options or choices that did not seem to be there in the first place.

Could Pain Be an Awareness Tool?

Let's consider something as apparently simple as a headache. The common approach to a headache is to take an aspirin or other pain-dulling medication. The good news is that the pain may well subside. The not-so-good news is that the source of the pain may still be there. Simply stated, what if pain serves as an awareness device that the body uses to make us aware of something that needs to be addressed? Dulling the pain may feel good in the moment, but it does nothing for the underlying cause or source of the pain.

By way of example, what if a headache were the result of emotional reactions, tension, or stress held in the body due to some circumstance needing to be addressed (difficult job, challenging relationship, fear about an upcoming change, etc.)? If the stressor continues unaddressed, the tension can build, leading to other, more serious complications, well beyond the reach of an aspirin.

What if the headache were an early warning tool, alerting you to the underlying tension or stress? If we ignore the pain (awareness device) long enough, then more serious consequences may begin to develop, perhaps something like hypertension or various gastrointestinal problems (ulcers anyone?).

The phrase *simple awareness can be curative* begins to take on new significance when viewed in this light.

We all know the definition of insanity as doing the same thing over and over again expecting a different result. The challenge lies in remaining unaware that we are doing the same thing over and over again—like taking that aspirin hoping that the issue will simply go away rather than looking for the source of the pain.

Did You Ever Burn Yourself on a Hot Stove?

Imagine you are in the kitchen and every time you are there, you feel intense, burning pain in your hand. I'm pretty sure you can see where we're heading—the pain comes from your hand touching the hot stove.

Once you become aware of the hot stove and the pain in your hand, you quickly modify your behavior when you're around the stove. How? By simply being aware that a hot stove can burn your hand. With that awareness, you then expand your field of awareness to notice if the stove is on and giving off heat. If it is, you don't have to run away from the kitchen, you simply know the source of potential pain and work around the source. With awareness, you can use the heat from the stove to your benefit without having to burn yourself.

If, on the other hand, you never noticed the association between a hot stove and the burning you feel in your hand, you might then declare the kitchen itself as the source of pain and the only option is to avoid the kitchen altogether.

Now I realize this example may seem simplistic at best. However, the world is full of people, me included, who have made incorrect associations and wound up avoiding what could be a source of great benefit—we just need to understand (become aware of) the true source of the pain. Ironically, by discovering the true source of the pain, we can wind up both liberated and pain-free.

Once we know the source of the pain in the stove example, we still need to stay awake/aware when we're in the kitchen! Sleepwalking around a hot stove is not a great idea.

Simultaneous Levels of Awareness

Awareness is something that develops over time, and something that can be applied in multiple settings, even at several layers of consciousness simultaneously. For example: Have you ever had the experience of talking with someone about something that you care about deeply only to notice that the other person isn't quite with you? That's a simple example of being aware of your own experience or process while simultaneously noticing what's happening with the other person.

You may also have had the experience of thinking about a project while also noticing how your body is feeling, perhaps hunger or tension or any other kind of sensation. That's another simple example of awareness at the mental level while simultaneously being aware of something at the physical level. We could substitute emotional awareness for physical and have the same idea.

Going back to the hot stove example, I'm sure you have found yourself in the kitchen along with someone else. You can hold a conversation with the other person, notice what you're thinking or feeling in that conversation all the while you are cooking on that hot stove, and even thinking a few steps ahead to the next thing you need to cook or prepare.

Again, a very simple, perhaps simplistic example of holding several levels of awareness at the same time. However, you probably needed some practice (experience) cooking before you could cook and hold that conversation at the same time.

CHAPTER 3

ACCEPTANCE

The first step toward change is awareness.
The second step is acceptance.

—Nathaniel Branden

For our purposes, acceptance simply means noticing what's present without denying or sugarcoating the situation. Your self-talk may be telling you that acceptance is nonsense because it equates acceptance with liking or agreeing with something. Acceptance can also imply a sense of resignation or feeling hopeless. When someone is in resignation, their self-talk might sound like: "*I don't like this and there's nothing I can do about it so why bother. I give up.*"

Your soul-talk may be reminding you that acceptance simply means to notice what is so.

If you're driving and get a flat tire, it won't do you any good to deny it's flat or declare the situation hopeless. Neither does acceptance suggest that you "like" the flat tire. Acceptance means acknowledging the reality of the situation which then opens up options or possibilities. Accepting that the tire is flat allows you to figure out what to do next—get out your spare, get someone to help, call for roadside assistance—different choices depending on the circumstances.

Acceptance, then, is the ability, even requirement, to acknowledge what is present so you can work with it.

It's Not What Happens to You, It's What You Do About It

My good friend W. Mitchell is a perfect example of acceptance, and I would like to share a bit of his story with you here. On July 19, 1971, Mitchell was burned over 65% of his body when a laundry truck turned in front of the motorcycle he was riding in San Francisco. His face was virtually burned off, and his hands were so badly burned that he lost most of each of his ten fingers.

After years of very painful convalescence, on November 11, 1975, the small plane he was piloting crashed on takeoff. He injured his spinal cord, leaving him paralyzed from the waist down, but his other passengers escaped injury.

Today he is a successful entrepreneur and one of the most sought-after motivational speakers in the world with a theme of *It's Not What Happens to You, It's What You Do About It*, which is also the title of his best-selling book. This powerful statement of his bears emphasis: "*Before I was paralyzed there were 10,000 things I could do. Now there are 9,000. I can either dwell on the 1,000 I've lost or focus on the 9,000 I have left.*" To me, Mitchell is a perfect example of acceptance leading to the cliché, when life gives you lemons, make lemonade. Only, it's not a cliché!

Your soul-talk is probably encouraging you to recognize acceptance as one of the major keys to life improvement. Once we come to terms with what is present, we can then begin to imagine and create choices that will allow us to move forward.

Are You Reading the Signs or Criticizing the Signpost?

Have you ever been tempted to "shoot the messenger" because you didn't like the message? If you're like me, you have probably received some kind of information or feedback that was accurate but also unpleasant to hear. If you're like me, your self-talk may have criticized the way the message was delivered as a way to avoid hearing (accepting) the message, much less do anything about the issue.

As I mentioned in the Introduction, early on in life, I became pretty adept at criticism as a way to keep others away. Even though I am more aware these days, my self-talk still tends to rush to the fore whenever I feel criticized, deflecting the feedback with criticism of my own. Not always, but still more frequently than I would like.

What's Eating You?

Imagine being in a relationship and the other person lets you know that he or she is unhappy in the relationship, that "you just don't listen." If the news gets your stomach going in knots, your self-talk may start finding fault with the other person. Hearing the feedback (criticism about not listening) may then stir up a number of feelings, perhaps ranging between hurt feelings and rejection over to resentment or guilt.

If you've been there, then you may have found yourself seeking solace in the form of food. You know the type—comfort food. For some people that means chicken soup and for others it means cake and ice cream in the unconscious hope that you will feel better as a result of eating. In a way, "eating about it" is akin to popping Excedrin for that headache.

I know I have crammed a goodly amount of cake and ice cream into my face only to wind up feeling even worse—the emotional upset is still there, along with whatever reasons it showed up, and now the body is feeling bad as well. (Ever heard the phrase, *something's eating at me?*) If this sounds familiar, rather than "eat about it" next time, perhaps a few minutes in meditation, in conversation with your true self, may prove much more useful.

What's going on with the "you just don't listen" feedback that led to "eating about it"? First, you heard some news that was upsetting. Of course, there may have been any number of cues earlier on that you just didn't pay attention to—like all the other times she told you that you just don't listen. Then there was this conversation in which you found yourself feeling hurt or scared. Perhaps it went something like this:

1. You heard some information (I'm unhappy in this relationship) and translated that to they're thinking of leaving me which then led to emotional upset or fear (self-talk: *Oh, no—I'll be all alone again*).

2. Then you started to notice some physical distress as the emotions kicked up around the stomach and you tightened up.

3. Then your self-talk started telling you that eating will help you feel better (which could go back to when you were a baby, crying because you were upset about something, and having Mom stick a bottle in your mouth, thus creating the association with feeling upset and resorting to food).

4. Then you felt even worse (upset stomach from food plus upset stomach from emotions).

In this example, we have several things going on simultaneously including mentally, emotionally, physically, and in the unconscious.

Does this sound even remotely familiar? If so, each of these levels of awareness could be accessed, in fact, need to be accessed, to both handle the current situation (upset) and learn from it, so you don't doom yourself to repeating it or wind up having your fear (being left) turn into reality.

If we could rewind the tape, back to when they first told you that "you just don't listen," your soul-talk probably noticed what they were saying and may have been encouraging you to take that in (acceptance), discover what that might be like for them, and find out what you do that comes across as not listening. Your soul-talk may have noticed the signs on the "signpost," but your self-talk was too busy criticizing the signpost.

Ignoring signs from the one you love or, worse yet, criticizing them for letting you know, are different forms of shooting the messenger.

All the while your soul-talk was hearing the words, your self-talk may have been translating them into something else, with a very different kind of meaning. Again, something unconscious could be going on here—you might have been hearing their words through the filters of what you heard growing up whenever Mom and Dad disagreed about something, or even how they avoided disagreeing. Whatever you heard back then, as well as observed about how they handled the situation, may have translated into an unconscious decision: *whenever I hear this kind of thing, it means. . . .* Our self-talk has an excellent memory for perceived threats, negativity, or shortcomings of any color or stripe.

Anywhere along the line, increased awareness of your soul-talk may have been sufficient for you to course-correct. If you had heard the original "you just don't listen" message and followed your soul-talk advice to understand what you just heard, rather than criticize the messenger, you may have looked underneath the feedback to examine your own behavior and reactions. From there, you might have discovered new choices about how to listen better, about how to engage more appropriately with your partner, or any number of other choices.

If you had noticed that your stomach was upset from emotional reactions to "you just don't listen," you might have accessed additional insights and choices, ranging from recognizing times when you don't listen to opening up to your partner in a way that builds intimacy. You may have noticed the built-in wiring code that told you the best response was to "eat about it."

The key notion here is that acceptance and awareness are required to perceive choices. If I am unaware, in denial, or otherwise blinded or deaf to what is going on inside, I may not be able to perceive choices, or even recognize the choices I am making (or denying). While *simple awareness can be curative*, it may not always be easy to open to or accept the awareness, especially if our self-talk is accustomed to being defensive or critical.

Where Are You Now?

The first step in any journey has to start with where you are (awareness), and so we will spend some time taking stock of your current life circumstances: what you have that you like, what you have that you don't like, and how you might like things to change.

Alice in Wonderland can be wonderfully instructive at this point. Paraphrasing with a bit of artistic liberty, when Alice told the Cheshire Cat that she didn't know where she wanted to get, the Cheshire Cat replied, "then any road will do." When Alice protested that she must get somewhere, the Cheshire cat replied, "and surely you will."

One of life's dilemmas centers around the distinction between what matters most and what I might be willing to accept, what I might be willing to settle for instead. To me, this notion of settling for something lesser is what Eric Hoffer was referring to when he wrote, "We can never have enough of that which we really do not want. What we want is justified self-confidence and self-esteem. If we cannot have the originals, we can never have enough of the substitutes."

This one can be quite subtle: sometimes I want something out of a sense of greed, sometimes out of if-only-I-had-then-I'd-be-OK, and sometimes it is something that truly matters at the deeper level of my true self.

To be clear, I'm not talking about something as prosaic as which car to drive (I settled for a fill-in-the-blank and I really wanted a fill-in-the-blank instead) or which trendy fashion to wear. What is it that truly matters deep inside of who I am, to my true self?

Problematically, our self-talk may be insistent about what we should want out of life, often based on what we may have heard from other people, ranging from our parents to the power of modern advertising. Our soul-talk, which is connected to our deeper wisdom, a kind of knowing that transcends beliefs and the opinions of others, speaks in a quieter voice, encouraging us to look past the objects of our desires and inquire into the deeper experience we may be seeking. As you continue reading, consider keeping a question in the back of your mind: where might I be settling for something less than what my true self is seeking?

CHAPTER 4

WEEVILS AND WHEELS—THE BANQUET TABLE OF LIFE

Start by doing what's necessary; then do what's possible;
and suddenly you are doing the impossible.

—Francis of Assisi

Try this mental exercise for a moment: imagine that you are kind of hanging out in life, with a handful of peanuts as your basic source of nutrition. However, these peanuts are also infested with weevils (a type of beetle). Appetizing, huh? How are you doing in terms of protein? With the peanuts, not bad. Even better if you consider the weevils. (I know, not the best humor, but it's what I have at the moment.)

As you find yourself moving through life with your peanuts and your weevils, you notice a banquet table in the not-too-far distance. Signs indicate that this is the "Banquet Table of Life." All that you could hope for in terms of your favorite foods, complete nutrition, and exquisite taste are right there. You are being invited to the table. YOU!

As you begin to approach the table, someone stops you, noticing the weevils in your hand, and says, "Wait just a minute. No weevily peanuts allowed at the Banquet Table of Life."

So, now what do you do? You could drop the peanuts and weevils, allow the weevils to scatter while the mice eat your peanuts, and proceed toward the banquet table. But your self-talk takes over: "What if this is an illusion? What if there is no banquet table? Or what if this is a joke, someone just teasing me? Or what if I get there and it's all been eaten? Or what if I am about to enter the banquet room and someone tells me that I'm not really welcome?"

Sound familiar? Our dreams are out there, but to bring them into reality, we may need to let go of what we currently have, what we are currently holding onto. However, the moment we let go, we may then experience the uneasy feeling of having nothing.

Have you already had the experience of letting go of something lesser while in search of something more fulfilling? If so, you may have also found that some friends or the world in general let you know that you must be crazy, that something must be wrong with your vision or goal. "Why would you give up that good paying job to pursue some pipe dream?" If this sounds familiar, you may also have noticed your self-talk right in there with those who would criticize your choice—"I told you this would be nuts."

About the time you consider letting go of something, one of life's interesting internal conflicts may emerge: "Well, it may not be much, but at least I know what I have." For some, that's as far as life ever gets—a bunch of weevily peanuts and stories about banquets that could have been.

In his 1936 classic, *Think and Grow Rich*, Napoleon Hill wrote, "No *more* effort is required to *aim high* in life, to demand abundance and prosperity, than is required to *accept misery* and *poverty*." Said differently, it takes no more energy to aspire to improved circumstances than it does to accept the weevily peanuts in life.

Reaching for the banquet table may require some degree of risk. Indeed, risk is real; however, as we will explore in Chapter 11 on Choice, you can choose to address the risk, create a strategy to mitigate the risk, and move forward—or—you can choose to stay where you are because, "the risk is just too great."

Have you ever wanted something, busted your tail to get it, and then wondered why you ever wanted it in the first place? If you're like me, then the answer is a resounding "yes!" The object of your desire could have been anything from a house, a car, an outfit, or even something seemingly more important like a certain job, a relationship, or most anything.

In this section, we will examine different aspects of life ranging from health and wealth to family and friends, from personal and spiritual growth to fun or adventure. As you review each area, you may discover that you are experiencing differing levels of satisfaction or fulfillment with what you have created or with certain choices you may have made along the way. Some areas may seem to be going better than others, some may seem like dreams fulfilled, while others may be less than ideal, something you have settled for along the way.

EXERCISE

The Wheel of Life—What Do You Want on Your Banquet Table?

Let's take a closer look at how you can begin making the transition from weevily peanuts to your own banquet table of life.

For the next piece to be effective, prepare a list of what you have accumulated so far in your life and then rank them in three tiers. Your list may include such things as jobs, career, or degrees; cars, houses, or bank accounts; friends, relationships, or social circles. The top tier represents those accomplishments or experiences you wouldn't trade for anything; the second tier includes items that are OK, but not great; and the third tier includes those circumstances that you would rather let go of in favor of something much more satisfying. Notice if any of these items on your list are your equivalent of the weevily peanuts, something you may have settled for rather than strived for.

The Wheel of Life is simply a way to graphically examine where you are in your life on several dimensions. See the next page for a first look at the Wheel:

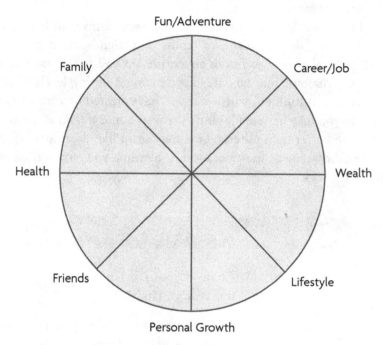

The Wheel of Life

Please feel free to re-label any of these spokes or dimensions. I have provided some of the more common areas I see in my coaching work. Other approaches to the wheel might include:

- *Roles you play in life.* Examples might include spouse, parent, manager, colleague, team member, coach, team leader, friend, family member, or breadwinner.

- *Areas of life important to you.* Examples might include artistic or creative expression, positive attitude, personal growth, spiritual growth, career, education, family, friends, financial freedom, physical challenge, pleasure, or public service.

- *Combination of roles and important areas.* Feel free to make this very personal, reflecting priorities or areas of interest.

To work with the Wheel, look at each dimension as though the center of the wheel represented zero and the outer edge of each "spoke" represented 100 in terms of how satisfied you are with each area.

The first step is to place a dot on the line somewhere between zero (the center) and 100 (the outer edge of the circle) representing your current level of satisfaction for each of the eight elements. For example, if you were completely satisfied with your health, then you would place the dot at the edge of the circle; if you were only 50% satisfied, then you would place the dot on the health line about half-way between the center of the circle and the outer edge. Do that for each of the eight elements.

Once you get all eight dots in place, go ahead and connect them. You might wind up with something that looks like this:

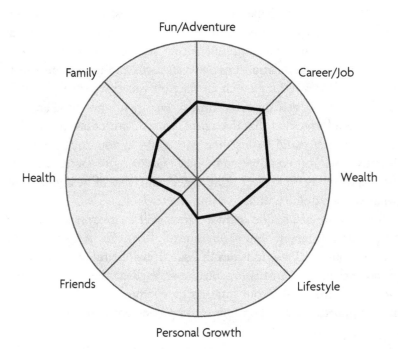

You can probably see why we call this the Wheel of Life. If your connected dots wind up forming something pretty irregular, something like one of the figures above, then imagine this misshapen wheel was on your car or your bicycle. How smooth would the ride be? Not very!

When the ride seems bumpy, what is your self-talk likely to say? Do any of these seem familiar:

- Who's responsible for maintaining this road?

- The car sure has a lousy suspension.

- I wish I had a new car, but I just can't afford it.

- Who am I kidding? I've tried to make this work before, and I keep coming up short. I'll never be able to get ahead.

What does the shape of your wheel suggest about where you place your focus compared to the outcomes or experiences you most desire? How much time and energy are you placing in the various areas? What is the relationship between focus and time spent working on each area to how much satisfaction you experience?

If you aren't placing much time or energy in one of the areas, it might stand to reason that the wheel is a little out of balance in that area. And that could be just fine with you—if you don't mind the bumpy ride. You could be consciously choosing to sacrifice family or friends in favor of career right now. Again, that's fine if you know what you are doing and don't mind the tradeoff.

For some of us, one or more areas will be sharply lower than others, and apparently out of our control. If you just lost your job or have encountered a serious health issue, it will be more than understandable that the area is low on the scale. Regardless of the situation, with Mitchell as our guiding light, your soul-talk may offer more opportunities and options for improvement than your self-talk might suggest.

The real question becomes: What can you do about any one of these areas? What can you do about the relative balance of the whole wheel?

The Myth of Balance

Given that we are working with the Wheel of Life, it would seem natural to assume that the goal is a perfectly balanced wheel. However, there's a clever illusion hiding here. The illusion? You could have a perfectly balanced wheel with every dimension coming in at five on a scale of 100. If all eight dimensions come in at five, then, indeed, you would have a perfectly balanced life of misery. Clearly, this version of balance is NOT the goal.

Balance is one of those illusive goals in life that seems ever so important and yet virtually unattainable. In my experience, balance is a myth, right along with its close cousin, stability.

In my consulting and coaching work, I have worked with countless people striving for greater balance and stability in life. Work-life balance continues to be a theme for many. (Notice that the lead word is almost always "work.") The emphasis on work is completely understandable, especially the way many of us had our self-talk programmed to get ahead, to work even harder, to "do better."

As companies pushed people to work harder, longer, to work virtually any time, anywhere, the stress on families and relationships has grown to unsustainable levels. Whole movements focused on creating "work-life" balance began proliferating in the 1980s. COVID-19 and Zoom fatigue have added to the stress and the need for "balance."

Wellness programs have proliferated focusing on "quality" over "quantity" with the emphasis on spending quality time with the family (so you won't feel bad about the quantity of time you were spending on work). Many companies have begun offering mindfulness and meditation training, many with altruistic intentions, helping people find greater (inner) balance.

While balance and stability seem desirable, the challenge lies in the implication that we can somehow arrive at a state that is balanced or stable, something static, that does not move or change. An admirable goal to be sure—just not something that maps to the real world.

Everything on this planet is in a state of change, even such big stable elements as the Rock of Gibraltar or Mount Everest. Sure, both are apparent "constants," and yet, both are in constant processes of change, albeit minute ones. Wind, rain, and the elements in general are causing each to change in small ways through erosion.

I understand the desire to seek stability. It's comforting to know that home is right where we left it, that the next paycheck is coming on time, and our relationships are dependable. However, jobs or job requirements change, the home needs attention, and relationships involve the ever-changing mental, physical, and emotional landscape of just being human. To be successful in any endeavor, rather than seek stability (which implies no change), it might be wiser to notice the signposts of change so we can adjust and adapt as necessary.

Balance is similar and even more tricky. Gymnastics, and the balance beam in particular, provide a great example of the conflict between the desire for balance and the myth that it is attainable. Good coaches will remind the gymnast that perfect (rigid) balance is not the goal—that would suggest the complete absence of movement. Instead, they teach the art of constant micro-correction, what I term "balancing."

Balancing requires great awareness and acceptance—the ability to notice what might be shifting and then to make the minor (or major) corrections necessary to remain "in balance."

The same is true in our personal or professional lives. We've all heard "change is the only constant" and yet rarely do we consider the implications of that while seeking stability and balance.

You may notice some areas of your wheel in which you are doing better than others and choose to focus your attention on an area needing greater attention. While attending to that spoke, you are in the process of making a "balancing adjustment." In the process, the "energy balance" may shift in other areas at the same time. It will be nearly impossible to achieve that mythological state of perfect balance, and yet you can be in a perfect state of "balancing."

Does this make sense to you? In my experience, creating greater fulfillment requires continuous awareness, noticing multiple dimensions of my life as I adjust my focus and activity from one to the other. While never achieving that mythological perfectly balanced, stable state, I am balancing just fine. Or perhaps I should say, re-balancing just fine.

Lopsided wheels seem to be normal, regardless of external conditions. The value of the wheel is to help us recognize where we might benefit from additional focus and work. You might ask yourself what your Wheel looks like now and what you would like it to look like a year from now.

With additional clarity on how you would like the Wheel to change, you can begin to make progress, realistic progress, in one or more areas. For example, let's imagine that you would like to improve your state of health. What would happen if you made improving your health a priority? Might it make a difference if you were to start exercising, even a little bit? How about five minutes? Three times a week? Once a day? As we will examine later in this book, even a simple "micro-step" like five minutes of exercise is enough to get yourself moving. Once you get yourself moving, you may discover that it is easier to keep moving, to do just a little bit more. In this way, slowly perhaps, you will begin to experience the kind of change you truly seek. It's not about going from "zero to hero," but making a bit of progress in your desired direction.

What if you want to improve your wealth? Could you imagine saving a dollar a week? Surely $52 won't mean you are wealthy, but it could mean that you're on the way. Once a dollar a week seems easy, it may be easier to move to a dollar a day. And and and. No matter the state of the economy, it will still be up to you to do what you can to improve your current situation. The same thing goes for any other area that seems out of balance—what can you do that might make a difference? Even a small difference?

As you reflect on each of your eight areas and imagine how you would like things to change over the next year, are there one or two areas that, if improved, would make a meaningful difference in how you experience your life? You don't have to have it all figured out yet in terms of how you will get there—you just need an image or vision of what improvement would look or feel like once you arrive.

Resist the temptation to dismiss this apparently simplistic advice by stating something so far removed from your current reality that anyone would dismiss the idea. If you are in debt, out of a job, and broke, it probably won't help to say that your goal is to become a billionaire by the end of the year. However, without a meaningful dream or imagination that's bigger than today, you won't find the motivation to do what you can to make a difference.

If you are holding onto some version of weevily peanuts, it will be difficult to find much inspiration, enthusiasm, fulfillment, or meaning in your life. And I'll bet you don't aspire to a handful of peanuts!

So, let's take the next step.

Get Up Off Your Dreams

If you can dream it, you can do it.

—WALT DISNEY

Each of us possesses the power to create life in much more expansive ways than we ever dreamed possible, yet sometimes, we may wind up settling for less, much less. And right there we have a great paradox: Dreaming isn't going to get us where we want to go, and yet if we don't allow ourselves to dream, there's no there to get to!

Sometimes, we won't allow ourselves to dream, because our self-talk keeps reminding us that dreaming seems so silly, so far away from reality, and just not worth the effort. Or it may be telling us that our dreams are just fantasies that can turn into nightmares if pursued. Who needs more nightmares in their life or yet another round of deep disappointment?

Your self-talk may remind you of times in the past when you allowed yourself to dream and then came crashing down to reality when you determined that you didn't have the power, strength, or skills necessary to make your dreams come true. It has evidence that dreaming doesn't work: *Just look at our life—how many of those dreams came true? No need to keep dreaming the impossible and winding up disappointed. After all, these peanuts aren't so bad, now, are they?*

I know I have had dreams and stopped short of engaging in the work necessary or become frustrated by imagining the seemingly inevitable roadblocks that can show up along the way. Self-doubt, self-criticism, and "stinking thinking" have been my biggest obstacles, often preventing me from even starting on the path. Does this seem familiar?

You may have had the opposite experience as well. Perhaps you started pursuing a goal or dream, tripped and fell, and then got up again and kept going. The secret is getting up one more time than you fall.

Dreaming doesn't work but working your dreams does. You have to get up off your dreams and start acting on them.

What Do You Want? Really?

"What do you want?" is one of those big questions in life, one that can be surprisingly difficult to answer. Or at least to answer in a way that is both sustaining and sustainable.

As Hoffer reminds us, *"We can never have enough of that which we really do not want. . . . and we run fastest and farthest from ourselves."*

The Dalai Lama has been "cited" many times on the Internet as having been asked what surprised him most about humanity. The Dalai Lama purportedly answered, "Man. Because he sacrifices his health in order to make money. Then he sacrifices his money in order to recuperate his health. And then he is so anxious about the future that he does not enjoy the present, the result being that he lives in neither the present nor the future; he lives as though he is never going to die, and then dies, having never really lived."

Curiously, there is no actual citation attributing this quote directly to His Holiness. For some, the lack of citation is enough to dismiss the inherent wisdom found here. For me and the purposes of this book, it does not matter if the Dalai Lama said this or not. If there's even a shade of truth or relevance here, then what does it matter who said it?

The real question to consider: Does this ring true for you? If so, what difference might it make if you listened more closely to the part of you that naturally knows when it hears the truth? You may notice two debates inside your head, one arguing that it's fluff and another, speaking in much quieter tones, encouraging you to consider how it applies to you and your life—not if it applies—but how it applies.

Symbols vs. Experience

Now that your wheel has given you a better picture of where you might place your focus, it might be helpful to ask a couple more clarifying questions of your true self, your soul-talk. As we dig into this, you may notice multiple answers coming up to simple questions about what you want out of life. Your self-talk may be working overtime to convince you that certain objects of your desire are more important than others.

In some ways, there will be a hierarchy to what you want. Abraham Maslow certainly shed some light on this when he wrote about the "hierarchy of needs" back in the 1940s and 1950s. He used the terms *physiological, safety, belonging and love, esteem,* and *self-actualization* to describe patterns or stages through which human behaviors typically move or evolve.

Clearly, if you need food, water, or shelter, then it will be difficult to focus on other levels such as relationships or self-esteem.

Keeping in mind that we do have differentiated needs, let's sharpen our focus here a bit more. As you look at the different spokes on your Wheel of Life, examine each area a bit more closely in two aspects: What do you want in each area and, perhaps more significantly, what is important about what you want—what's the purpose, "the why" you want it?

When I say "why" you want something, I'm not asking for a list of "logical" reasons, explanations, or defenses. Instead, consider what you are hoping to experience if you had "enough" of whatever each spoke represents for you.

In the parlance of this exercise, let's look at the Symbols of what you want and compare those to the Experiences you hope to have as a result. In many ways, Eric Hoffer was referring to the Symbols when he wrote, *you can never get enough of what you don't truly want.*

For each spoke of your wheel, spend some time completing the following *Symbols vs. Experience* exercise to clarify what you want out of each area and why it is important to you. Your self-talk may already be niggling you here: *What on earth is he going on about. It's pretty darn clear why we want more money, a better job, etc.* However, your soul-talk may be quietly *encouraging* you to take a deeper look.

(By the way, the obvious root word of encourage is "courage." Most people think courage has something to do with bravery, bravado, or fearlessness. If you look at the etymology of the word, you will find that it comes from the Latin and French for heart. The suffix "age" stems from the Latin *sapere* meaning to have good taste or to be wise. Courage, then, really means to "have the wisdom of the heart." And where does your soul-talk reside? The heart, of course. As we delve into this, let's keep the mind [self-talk] and heart [soul-talk] equally present so we can discern the practical as well as the deeper levels of experience or meaning you are after in life. Your soul-talk may be encouraging you to look more deeply inside.)

How to Know What You Truly Want

In the following exercise below, complete the left-hand column of the table for each spoke of your wheel. The left-hand column labeled "Symbols" represents the tangible things people often focus on in life hoping for something even better to follow. I call this "*if only thinking*." "If only I had (a certain amount of) money." "If only I had the right house, new car, better job, etc." For some people, even relationships can be relegated to the level of thing or Symbol—think of those people who strive for the perfect "trophy" relationship—not for the quality of the relationship, but for advantages they hope will follow.

The point here is to delineate as truthfully as you can, that which you find yourself focusing on in life, those *things* you want or want more of. These *things* go in the left-hand column.

SYMBOLS	EXPERIENCE
Money or Wealth	
House	
Health	
Toys (golf clubs, boats, etc.)	
Travel	
Perfect Relationship	
Job	
Career	
Etc.	

From here, spend a little time reflecting on the question: "Why do I want those things?" "What do I hope will be true if I have the (job, money, house,)?" A slightly more refined question would be: "what *experience* am I looking for"—if I had the right car, house, money, what would I be *experiencing*?" Do your best to engage your soul-talk in the conversation. Look past the easy and obvious self-talk retort: *of course, I want more money because then I could buy more things, take better vacations, etc.*

Most people I have worked with would say they want more money. When I ask them why, or what more money would do for them, I usually hear variations on the theme of things they could buy, trips they could take, etc. However, I then ask them to think a bit more deeply on the question of experience. "What positive *experience* or experiences would you associate with having more money?"

So That

Another way to approach the distinction between the left- and right-hand columns is to insert this little phrase *so that* between the two columns—I want (fill in the blank) *so that* I can experience (fill in the blank). This one often takes several rounds of repetition before the deeper meaning, the deeper *so that* becomes clear.

What are those *so that experiences* that your true self is seeking? As you review your Symbols column, let your soul-talk provide the answers and then place those so that experiences in the right-hand column. It might look something like the figure on the next page.

In that figure, money is one answer to the question "What do you want?" When I ask, what positive so that experiences are associated with having enough money, most people respond with something along the lines of wanting greater freedom, security, sense of power or accomplishment, and peace of mind. I then ask: "Do you know anyone with a lot of money who doesn't have much freedom, security, or peace of mind?" Howard Hughes would be a classic example of someone who had loads of cash and not much freedom, security, or peace of mind.

SYMBOLS	EXPERIENCE
Money & Wealth	Freedom
Health	Security
House	Fun
Car	Excitement
Toys (golf clubs, boats, etc.)	Happiness
Travel	Love
Perfect Relationship	Peace of Mind
Job	Success
Career	

Of course, you can always ask the question the other way around. "Do you know anyone who does not have much money and yet experiences freedom, security, and peace of mind?" Mother Teresa would have been an example on this side of the coin.

And, just to keep it real, there are people with lots of money who are free, secure, and at peace and those without money who aren't free, secure, and at peace. The two important questions: What do I really want and how do I get there?

If it's true that "You can never get enough of what you don't really want," then it may pay to dig deeper into what it is that you truly want.

If you are looking for the experience of being secure, free, and at peace, is there any amount of money (or house, or car, or perfect relationship) that will produce those experiences?

The obvious implication here is, "NO!"

What do you truly want and how do you produce it? Is it the Symbols of life that you truly want or is it the Experiences found in the right-hand column?

If you are like me, the answer is "BOTH!" The main point here is to make certain we know the *why* we want something, not just the *what*. While the emphasis here is on the right-hand column of experience, the left-hand column can be important as well.

Most people believe that the left-hand column has a causal relationship with the right-hand column—a large enough supply of money yields the experience of success, happiness, security, etc.

If that were true, not only would "rich" people feel that way, but all rich people would. And no "poor" person would.

And we all know that isn't true.

Even the songs say so: *Can't buy me love.*

In my own life, I have drifted back and forth from "wouldn't a bigger house be great" over to "any roof over my head is enough." While it may be true that any roof is enough, and I don't *need* a bigger house, I do find that my preferences can make a difference on many levels of life. However, I have learned that there is no amount of "better, bigger house/bank account/career" that will produce the inner experiences I truly seek.

So, let's spend a bit more time on the right-hand column. The hypothesis here is that your self-talk will keep you focused on pursuing the left-hand column in hopes of one day experiencing the right-hand column.

What if it is the right-hand column that your true self wants, and yet your self-talk persists in telling you that you must defer what you truly want while you pursue all the things in your left-hand column? What if fulfilling the right-hand column resulted in your self-talk quieting as it realizes the source of true satisfaction?

If this makes any sense at all, then let's work from the notion that the right-hand column is what you're after, what your soul-talk is guiding you toward, and that you can produce those experiences regardless of life's circumstances.

I invite you to keep Mitchell in mind here. You may not be badly burned or paralyzed, and yet you may be "handicapping" yourself simply through your self-talk.

If what you want is freedom, peace of mind, security, a sense of fullness or completion, and you had freedom, peace of mind, security, and a sense of fullness or completion in your life, would it matter how much money you have?

Wait a minute. Is this a trick question?

Well, yes and no. I have found that the more I focus on the positive experiences I want out of life, not only do I tend to produce those more frequently but also the easier it is to produce the things found on the left-hand side of the equation. Focusing on money hasn't made me any more secure or free, yet focusing on producing freedom and security has made it easier to create material success to go along with those inner qualities of success.

Again, have you ever told yourself that you really, really wanted something, worked hard on getting it, got it, and then found you weren't any happier? That's a common experience when we follow the louder voice of our self-talk, which may have been influenced by the opinions of other people about what "should" be important, rather than the deeper wisdom of our soul-talk. If this seems familiar, my suggestion would be to spend more time focusing on creating what you really want in the right-hand column, on your so that experiences. You may find it worthwhile to revisit the right-hand column frequently, each time digging a little deeper. In doing so, you may find deeper meaning as you continue to ask: "*What do I really want?*"

After all, can you ever get enough of what you don't really want?

CHAPTER 5

PURPOSE AND VISION

The real voyage of discovery lies in seeing with new eyes.

—Marcel Proust

Much has been written about purpose and vision, so much so that the distinction and value of the two have become blurred in many people's minds. For this book, purpose refers to *the underlying reason you do something, want something, or pursue something*—the deeper *so that experiences* we seek—while vision refers to the sense or image of what it would be like if the purpose were fulfilled.

I also resonate with the additional layer of insight Merriam-Webster provides in defining vision as *a supernatural appearance that conveys a revelation.*

If we combine all of these, purpose and vision become the inspiration and guidance from our true self.

Desired Outcome

Focusing on purpose and vision helps clarify what it is that we are truly striving toward in life, both in terms of material success as well as our deeper level of experience. Together, these represent what I call our *desired outcome.* If it all went well, what would you have at the end? Not only what would you have accomplished physically, but what experience would you have along the way?

Putting life together in a way that is both meaningful and

fulfilling is a lot like putting a jigsaw puzzle together. For most of us, pieces of the puzzle called life show up much like a puzzle fresh out of the box, scattered somewhat randomly, rarely in perfect order.

Trying to make sense out of what appear to be random pieces can be challenging. Putting the puzzle together can be especially difficult if you don't have a picture of the finished puzzle to begin with. Fortunately, most puzzles come with pictures on the box. If only it were so with the puzzle of life.

"Desired outcome" is the puzzle picture on the outside of the box. We get to create that picture ourselves.

If You Don't Know Where You Are Going, Any Road Will Do

Many years ago, a friend and mentor of mine watched me struggle with making sense out of my life. I had been dabbling in various life experiments (work, education, career, meaning of life, etc.) and only found myself being frustrated. One day, Ernie reminded me that, "if you don't know where you are going, any road will do" is more than a cliché—it's a prerequisite to a satisfying and fulfilling life.

To me, this simple aphorism has become central to making effective choices in my life. If I don't know where I'm going, and I come to a fork in the road, how do I know which fork to take?

The earlier reference to Alice in Wonderland underscores the challenge many face when the road forks in life. Have you ever felt like Alice lost in a maze of options, looking for your version of the Cheshire Cat to tell you which way to turn? Ernie's observation reflected the simple yet profound wisdom of the Cheshire Cat—if Alice didn't know where she wanted to get, *then any road would do.* Just as Alice protested that she must get somewhere, the Cheshire Cat's snide but accurate reply fits equally well, *and surely you will.* All roads lead somewhere.

In my own life, as well as in helping other people discover and evaluate their own choices, it's become clear that many of us come across those forks in the road without a clear idea of our desired outcome. When that happens, all too often our self-talk response can be something along the lines of, "Oh well, it doesn't matter, just pick one." And a bit later we come to another fork in the road. Which one should we take? Again, who knows, or it doesn't matter, or just tell me which one to take, or any of a dozen other muddled responses.

Sooner or later, this series of choices about which fork to take leads somewhere. Do I like where I find myself or do I complain about my circumstances or even wind up blaming someone else for the results?

"Why me?" "How did this happen?" "Where did this come from?" These are the kinds of plaintive questions my self-talk can bemoan when I fail to realize that I am the one who made the choices at each fork in the road.

My self-talk is pretty good at assigning blame for my own choices. If I don't like where the road took me, what or who does my self-talk blame? The road, of course! Or the signpost. Or the Cheshire Cat.

So, let's back up a bit. Imagine that you do know where you are going. You have a destination in mind. You find yourself moving down life's path when you come to a fork. Which one should you take? Does it matter? The only time it doesn't matter is when you don't care where you are heading. In this instance, you do care and you do have a destination or outcome in mind.

Now as you find yourself standing at the fork, ask yourself, "If I am trying to get to my desired outcome, which fork seems more likely to get me there? What would my soul-talk advise?" With that little bit of guidance, you can now make a somewhat more informed choice without that nagging self-talk holding you back or sending you down another road to nowhere.

Does this mean that we will have chosen correctly? By no means, no! However, having chosen *toward* our desired outcome, we can now observe more clearly what happens next. If data or experience appear along the way, indicating that we have chosen incorrectly, what can we do?

One choice would be to return to the previous fork in the road and try the other one. Another option would be to notice where we are now and look for other, more immediate choices that might help us get back on track.

Any of these options are possible and potentially effective. The key element is knowing what direction you are heading, where you are now, and what is your desired outcome. It probably goes without saying, but just in case, consulting your soul-talk, your true self, can make a huge difference.

Even when things are going well, you might also consider asking yourself: *As good as my life is now, could it be even better?* I love the notion of *good and getting better.*

MEDITATION EXERCISE

Good and Getting Better

This meditation is a variation of the practice we introduced in Chapter 1. This kind of awareness-focused meditation can be adapted to many issues that arise in life. Please feel free to modify what follows to work well for you and whatever question or questions you may have in mind.

Begin with a breathing or relaxing practice that works for you. Some find it helpful to imagine they are in a peaceful place in nature, undisturbed by the day-to-day world. Others prefer to focus on their heart. There's no wrong way to do this, so just let yourself find your own relaxing, safe space and follow your own rhythm.

Invite your true self to come forward (feel free to substitute your inner master, your soul, or any other representation of deeper awareness that works for you).

- Remaining in this quiet state, consciously invite that quieter part of you, your true self, to come forward as though it were sitting or standing in front of you. At first, you may not notice much difference, at least not in your body, mind, or emotions. You may simply feel more peaceful.

You may notice or sense a presence, and some will even "see" a more clearly defined form, perhaps even an image of yourself.

- As you begin to get a sense of this inward presence, ask it to bring back to you a time or times in your life when you felt grateful, fulfilled, or at peace. Allow images, thoughts, or feelings to emerge—they could be from your distant past or quite recent.

- Ask this inner presence to help you identify an area of your life that you would like to experience as *good and getting better.*

- Feel free to make this more like a conversation with a trusted friend—pretty much a free-form exchange. Your soul-talk may have questions for you, ideas to consider, or suggestions for new options.

- If you hear something that you don't quite understand, ask for clarification.

- Be sure to repeat what you are hearing and how you imagine it can be implemented. Then ask if you heard correctly.

- Once you and your true self feel complete, thank your true self for its support and guidance, and return to your breathing process.

- When you are ready, slowly allow your eyes to open and focus back into the room where you find yourself.

- Write down what you heard.

CHAPTER 6

LIVING AN INSPIRED LIFE—WHERE ARE YOU HEADING AND WHY?

*If you do not change direction, you may
wind up where you are headed.*

—Lao Tzu

Is That All There Is?

I have worked with thousands of people over the years who are otherwise successful and yet seem to lack much genuine excitement, inspiration, or enthusiasm in their lives. Regardless of their material successes and the excitement that comes from knocking off goals, their inner experience can sometimes be somewhere between dull and boring to depressing. Sooner or later, this kind of experience can be summed up in that familiar plaintive cry, "Is that all there is?"

Of course, everything could be just fine in your life and still have room for improvement. Counter to much of western thinking, we don't have to be sick to get better. My basic premise is that each of us is doing fine considering where we are right now, and that each of us could be doing even better. Perhaps all that is missing is a dose of inspiration, enthusiasm, or deeper meaning.

According to freedictionary.com, an inspired life is one "of such surpassing brilliance or excellence as to suggest divine inspiration."

They go on to say that the word inspire means "to communicate or suggest by a divine or supernatural influence: To affect, guide, or arouse by divine influence."

Sometimes life can feel uninspired, or at least under-inspired. Princeton University's WordNet 3.1 defines uninspired as "having no intellectual, emotional, or spiritual excitement; dull" and uninspiring as "depressing to the spirit." This could also describe a life lacking enthusiasm.

Inspiration, Aspiration, and Enthusiasm

Inspiration, aspiration, and enthusiasm are important terms for understanding the deeper messages from your true self and the work that follows, so please allow me to dig into their deeper meaning.

The etymology of inspiration and aspiration reveals that they share a common lineage, all stemming from a 13th-century root word, *inspirare*, meaning an animating or vital principle, from old French and Latin words meaning soul, courage, and breath.

According to wordreference.com, the word *inspire* means:

- to fill with an animating, quickening, or exalting influence

- to communicate or suggest by a divine or supernatural influence

- to guide or control by divine influence.

Merriam-Webster.com provides additional context for the original meaning of inspire:

> When inspire first came into use in the 14th century it had a meaning it still carries in English today: "to influence, move, or guide by divine or supernatural influence or action."

The meaning is a metaphorical extension of the word's Latin root: inspirare means "to breathe or blow into." The metaphor is a powerful one, with the very breath of a divine or supernatural force asserted as being at work.

The Inspirational History of Inspiration

Inspiration has an unusual history in that its figurative sense appears to predate its literal one. It comes from the Latin inspiratus (the past participle of inspirare, "to breathe into, inspire") and in English has had the meaning "the drawing of air into the lungs" since the middle of the 16th century. This breathing sense is still in common use among doctors, as is expiration ("the act or process of releasing air from the lungs"). However, before inspiration was used to refer to breath it had a distinctly theological meaning in English, referring to a divine influence upon a person, from a divine entity; this sense dates back to the early 14th century. The sense of inspiration often found today ("someone or something that inspires") is considerably newer than either of these two senses, dating from the 19th century.

Multiple dictionaries tell us that aspire and aspiration share the same Latin root, *inspirare*. Merriam-Webster follows the theme, suggesting that aspiration means "a strong desire to achieve something high or great."

Whereas common usage has reduced an aspiration to an ordinary goal or ambition, I prefer to think about Aspiration as something that comes with a capital "A," meaning a goal with a bit more capital "I" Inspiration than a more mundane day-to-day goal.

Following from the earlier origins of the word, an *Inspired Life* would be one wherein meaning or motivation come from divine influence or Spirit. An *Aspirational Life* would mean seeking to lead a Spirit-led life, a soul-centered life, one of higher purpose and meaning.

Living a life of inspiration and aspiration can be characterized by enthusiasm and a pervading sense of well-being. We're not talking about that kind of bubbly energy that appears positive and yet winds up being shallow or dogmatic. Genuine, authentic enthusiasm emanates from who you truly are, from your spiritual source.

Once again, the etymology of the word is helpful. Enthusiasm comes from the Greek, "en + theos" or "in God." Therefore, if someone is truly enthusiastic, they would be infused or imbued with some connection to Spirit or the Divine. Enthusiasm also shares a similar etymological root with inspiration and aspiration.

Merriam-Webster provides more on the history of the word: "Enthusiasm entered the English language around the beginning of the 17th century. It was borrowed from the Greek enthousiasmos, meaning 'inspiration or possession by a god.'"

Do You Aspire to a Life of Inspiration and Enthusiasm?

The difference between a so-so humdrum existence and greater fulfillment, abundance, meaning, and inspiration may seem monumental in some ways, perhaps out of reach, and yet the keys are simple, elegant, and available to everyone.

To experience the deeper sense of meaning and fulfillment that your true self may be seeking, questions like these may arise:

- How do you reconcile life goals with aspirational goals?

- How do you work with goals of the ordinary kind—career, wealth, etc.—while also maintaining a focus on the inner guidance from your soul?

- How do you accomplish goals without sacrificing that sense of deeper meaning?

- How do you integrate divinely inspired guidance with day-to-day reality?

Ask yourself:

- How fulfilled do you find yourself these days?

- Can you imagine living an even more fulfilling life, or is it enough to just get by?

- Are you inspired by your life? By what you do? By who you are?

- Do you wish you could be more inspired?

As you consider the answers to these provocative questions, notice who is answering. Is it your self-talk or your soul-talk?

If this idea of noticing who is answering seems a bit odd, you might consider these questions:

- Have you ever thought a thought that you wished you weren't thinking? If so, who noticed?

- Have you ever felt a feeling that you wished you weren't feeling? If so, who noticed?

You did, of course. So how could "you" have a thought or feeling "you" wished "you" weren't thinking or feeling? Who is the "you" that noticed? What if it is the deeper you, the one beyond the criticisms, doubts, and fault-finding? What if it is your true self, your soul-talk, patiently waiting to be noticed and known?

Are Dreams Aspirational Signposts?

As we pointed out in Chapter 4 of this book, dreams alone aren't going to get us where we truly want to go, and yet if we don't allow ourselves to dream, there's no there to get to! If you listen closely to your dreams, even your daydreams, you may find your soul-talk quietly inspiring you to achieve something of even greater purpose and meaning in your life. If so, it may also be encouraging you to *get up off your dreams and start acting on them.*

Often, our self-talk won't allow us to dream, much less follow those dreams. Self-talk can be all too familiar, telling us to "get real," admonishing us those dreams are just fantasies that can come crashing down to reality when the inevitable roadblocks or obstacles show up. If you have had this experience, you may have found your self-talk reminding you that you didn't have the power, strength, resources, or skills necessary to make your dreams come true.

Have you ever shared your dreams with someone else only to have them tell you to "wake up," suggesting that you are being unrealistic, living in a fantasy world, and needing to "get real"?

Great advice! Awakening is a good thing, but it doesn't mean giving up your dreams. It means awakening from the dream and then translating that bit of inspiration into an aspiration that you, and you alone, have the power to make happen. Perhaps a dream is your true self encouraging you to awaken to that which truly matters in your life, awakening from the lesser dreams of the material world and moving into the more expansive dreams of leading a soul-centered life.

This might be another good time to invite your soul-talk to review your Wheel of Life and your Symbols vs. Experience list for additional guidance.

What is your true self, your soul-talk, inspiring you toward? Are there higher-level goals, aspirational goals, that can help you shift your Wheel in ways both quantitative as well as qualitative?

An aspirational goal may be something that you aspire to, with its actual achievement being of little or no importance. Why? Because a key element of an aspirational goal is to live by and through the inspiration that comes from aligning with your true self, your soul.

You may have heard the old cliché about "life is a journey, not a destination." Indeed, the focus here is more on the quality of experience you have as you go through life than it is on any physical or material scorecard. However, you can have a measure of both—quality, fulfilling, enriching life experience coupled with the ability to create more of what you seek in the physical world as well.

If you aspire to that kind of journey, it may be helpful to examine what your self-talk has to say and how to bring your true self, your soul-talk, into the conversation.

EXERCISE

Building Positive Self-Talk

Start by describing a goal for some aspect of your Wheel that could stand improving. It could be anything from changing careers to building up your savings or improving your health.

Once you have a goal in mind, create a two-column chart of different messages your self-talk and soul-talk might have about your dreams or aspirations. Keep this one handy because you may find it useful when we get to the section on affirmations and visualizations you can use to create more of what you truly prefer in life.

SELF-TALK	SOUL-TALK
You're never going to make this work.	I'm creative and I can find a way.
Why bother? People like us never succeed.	I can always improve.
You idiot!	I'm a good person who makes mistakes.
The road ahead is just too difficult.	I only need to take one step at a time.
Are you kidding? You have no idea how to do this.	Of course I can—I just need to learn a bit more.

CHAPTER 7

INTENTION AND FOCUS: ENERGY FOLLOWS THOUGHT

The universe doesn't give you what you ask for with your thoughts—it gives you what you demand with your actions.

—Steve Maraboli

Now that your Wheel and Symbols vs. Experiences exercises have given you a better idea of what you want out of life and why it matters to you, let's look more deeply into the process of creating what you want. As you will see, this also applies to how you may wind up creating what you don't want.

I'm sure you have heard the old but still true cliché that doing the same thing over and over again expecting a different result is pretty much the definition of insanity. Marshall Goldsmith very eloquently captures an entire life lesson in the title of his best-selling book, *What Got You Here Won't Get You There.* If what we have been doing up until now were going to produce a different result, it would have already taken place!

Simply stated, it comes down to focus. Where we focus, we tend to go.

I'm pretty sure you know this to be true in so many ways. It can be as simple as the old country wisdom you've probably heard a thousand times, but maybe didn't notice what it was saying, "just follow your nose." If you drive a car or ride a bike, you will know that where you look is where you tend to go—your nose is pointing the way as it were.

We tend to create what we focus on and then focus on what we create. Your self-talk can show you the negative application of this: "things (like this) never work out for me." Or "this is too good to be true." Or any of a dozen similar predictions of things going south. As soon as our self-talk reminds us of all the times things didn't go well in the past, our focus tends to go that way, right here, right now. Funny how where we look today tends to create our future—we travel the path of our focus.

The Neuroscience of Focus

When you are focused on your priorities, what you have determined is truly in your highest self-interest, the other things can drop away, including possessions and obsessions. Your focus is like your intention: Where are you going? That's up to you to decide because it's your life.

—JOHN-ROGER, DSS

Focus engages a part of your brain called the reticular formation and the reticular activating system (RAS). For our purposes, allow me to provide a rather rudimentary explanation and an example or two of how it works in everyday life.

One way to view the RAS is to think of it as a filter. When we focus on something, the RAS tends to screen *in* information that supports our area of focus while simultaneously blocking or screening *out* anything unrelated.

Try this one right where you are. What's the dominant color in the room where you are now? Did you have to look around first? Not surprising if you did—while reading this, or doing most anything, color is relatively unimportant. Unless of course you're a designer, painter, or engaged in some activity where color is important. So, let's say that the dominant color is off-white for the moment—please do substitute whatever your dominant color happens to be.

Now look around the room and see if you can find red—any instance of red will do, no matter how small or insignificant. Feel free to choose blue or any other color. While you are noticing red, where did off-white go? Obviously, it didn't go anywhere, but did you notice that while looking for red, your brain tended to screen out off-white?

That's a very simple example of how the RAS functions. There are other ways it works as well, lots of them. Let's imagine you're about to go into a meeting where someone you don't particularly care for will also be in attendance. Your self-talk may remind you of all the times things didn't go well with this person; in fact, it may tell you something like, "that guy's a jerk." Now you have programmed your reticular system to find proof that "he's a jerk." Sure enough, you'll start to notice behaviors that you don't appreciate and again assign the label "jerk." Have you ever had someone whom you admire tell you after the meeting that the person you labeled a jerk was fabulous, brilliant, or otherwise decidedly un-jerk-like?

Consider the experience of Mitchell as he recovered from those burns and paralysis. He could have told himself that he was victimized beyond all hope and resigned himself to a life of limited opportunity and success. Few of us would have faulted him had he so chosen. Had he focused on being helpless or limited, imagine what might have become his reality.

Instead, in his own words: "Before I was paralyzed there were 10,000 things I could do. Now there are 9,000. I can either dwell on the 1,000 I've lost or focus on the 9,000 I have left."

By choosing to focus on the 9,000 he had left and how he could optimize his situation, he became one of the world's foremost motivational speakers, enjoying a life of health, wealth, and happiness. He just happened to be a healthy, wealthy, and happy paraplegic with significant burn scars.

Why Positive Thinking Just Doesn't Work

Back when I was a senior editor at the Huffington Post, I published a couple hundred articles on various aspects of conscious living, following a theme of "how to create the life you want instead of the one you might have settled for." The Internet trolls had a field day with me, blasting me for publishing a bunch of "positive thinking pablum," labeling me a snake oil salesman, and making a range of other dismissive attacks.

I wrote several articles addressing the criticisms, none of which did much other than fuel their fires. Then one morning, as I was preparing my next article, a new approach showed up in the form of the title, "Why Positive Thinking Just Doesn't Work."

That article went viral with thousands of people reading it and passing it along to others.

The basic message: *of course, positive thinking doesn't work. Positive action does. But how do you take positive action without first having a positive focus?*

People who miss the point dismiss positive thinking as living in a fantasy world, that positive thinking is akin to pretending something negative is somehow good. Surely Mitchell wasn't thinking to himself, "now isn't this great. My face is burned off, my fingers gone and now I'm paralyzed. Perfect. Couldn't be better."

Far from it. Mitchell had to move into acceptance and recognize the truth of the situation. The truth was simply a collection of facts—burns, missing fingers, paralysis. However, the truth did not include negative interpretations or self-defeating limitations. Despite his apparent limitations, he chose not to be limited by them.

He had a choice. He could focus on the limitations and wind up "paralyzing" himself beyond the paralysis. Or he could focus on what he could do despite, or even because of, the limitations.

Had he chosen to focus on what he had lost, goodness knows where he might have wound up. However, by focusing on what he could do, he created an abundant, rewarding life, beyond what many "able-bodied" people would dare to imagine for themselves.

Where would your true self have you focus? What does your self-talk have to say about it?

There's Only One Energy

Everything is energy and that is all there is to it. Match the frequency
of the reality you want and you cannot help but get that reality.
It can be no other way. This is not philosophy. This is physics.

—ALBERT EINSTEIN

If you're on board with awakening, awareness, and acceptance, let's examine what may be two of the most important takeaways from this book: *There's only one energy* and *energy follows thought.*

As anyone who has studied physics will tell you, the universe is made of energy. Whether we're looking at a rock, another person, or anything else, it's all just energy in different forms. You probably already know that you can't create energy, nor can you destroy energy. Albert Einstein put it this way: "Energy cannot be created or destroyed; it can only be changed from one form to another."

What you can do, however, is change its form and direct its course. Electricity coming from sun rays, turbines spun by wind, water or steam, or any other source, are examples of taking one form of energy and transforming it into another form.

In essence, there's only one energy and it's neutral regarding how you choose to apply it. Much like a hammer which can be used to drive a nail or crush your thumb, energy is there for you to use. You can use the energy available to you to create, destroy, deny, or just about anything you want.

Stay with me here—I know this may be a bit circuitous, and I'm confident you will find enormous value by following this through.

Information Is Universal and Universally Available

Are you listening to BBC radio right now? Or ABC? Or any other radio frequency? Probably not. But, if you're not listening to the BBC while reading this, does that mean that the BBC is NOT in the room or wherever you happen to be?

The radio signal is there all right, you're just not hearing it. Why not? Because you're not a radio of course. However, if you were to turn on a radio, you could then tune it to the BBC frequency and listen to whatever is being broadcast right now. The same applies to any other radio or television channel. You just need to have a tuner and attune to the station to hear or see what's being broadcast.

Radio and television signals are different forms of that one, universal energy. Early "wireless" pioneers figured out how to manipulate that energy into an invisible "form" or frequency and broadcast it so that those who are "attuned" could hear it. Television works the same way—that "one energy" is formed in such a way that both auditory and visual information are broadcast over the "airwaves." (Chapter 8, "Learning to See the Invisible," will dive into this notion even more deeply.)

What If You Are Both the Tuner and the Broadcaster?

*We are souls dressed up in sacred biochemical garments
and our bodies are the instruments through which
our souls play their music.*

—ALBERT EINSTEIN

Similarly, your soul-talk is both a frequency and a tuner. Your soul-talk happens to be attuned to a higher frequency emanating from a source more profound than any radio station or broadcaster.

Fortunately, you don't need a radio or any external device to attune to the frequency emanating from and through your soul. As it turns out, *you are the tuner!* It may take some practice before you can readily attune to the inner frequency and hear the messages coming from your deeper source. However, if you practice, not only can you attune, but you can also get better and better as you go along—perhaps to the point that you can hear the soul-talk even amid the louder, more insistent self-talk.

Many forms of meditation can help us access the deeper messages coming through our soul-talk. You could try anything from mindfulness to simply sitting quietly asking your soul what messages it might have for you. For ease of reference, here's the simple meditation we first introduced in Chapter 1.

Soul-Talk Meditation Practice

We will begin with the box breathing technique. From there, we will suggest that you focus inwardly and invite your true self to come forward. We will then pose some questions and engage in a bit of dialogue with your true self or soul-talk. When you feel complete, you can simply repeat the box breathing technique and return to your more conscious, awake state.

Before starting, sit with your back supported in a comfortable chair and your feet on the floor.

Box Breathing

1. Close your eyes and breathe in through your nose while counting to four slowly. Notice the air entering your lungs.

2. Now gently hold your breath inside while counting slowly to four. Try not to clamp your mouth or nose shut. Simply avoid inhaling or exhaling for another count of four.

3. Next, slowly and gently exhale for another count of four.

4. At the bottom of the fourth count, pause and hold for a count of four.

5. Repeat steps one to four at least three times. Ideally, repeat them for four minutes, or until you feel deeply relaxed or calm.

Invite your true self to come forward (feel free to substitute your inner master if you prefer, or your soul).

- Some find it helpful to imagine they are in a peaceful place in nature, undisturbed by the day-to-day world. Others prefer to focus on their heart. There's no wrong way to do this, so just let yourself find your own relaxing, safe space and follow your own rhythm.

- Remaining in this quiet state, consciously invite that quieter part of you, your true self, to come forward as though it were sitting or standing in front of you. At first, you may not notice much difference, at least not in your body, mind, or emotions. You may simply feel more peaceful. Some will notice a presence, and some will even "see" a more defined form, perhaps even an image of yourself.

- As you begin to get a sense of this inward presence, tell it what you have been thinking about or considering, literally "speaking" to it as though it were physically in the room with you right now. You might want to start with an area of your life that needs attention or some choice you are considering. Let your true self know what you have been thinking, perhaps some limiting, critical aspect of your self-talk. Ask your true self or soul-talk what it would prefer that you notice or focus upon. Or you might want to ask your true self for its recommendations about a different choice you could consider making about where you are in your life right now.

- Feel free to make this more like a conversation or free-form exchange with a trusted friend. Your soul-talk may have questions for you, ideas to consider, or suggestions for new options. Sometimes, your true self will be direct with its advice or preferences. Rarely will the tone be harsh; rather, it most likely will be loving, supporting, and nurturing.

- If you hear something that you don't quite understand, ask for clarification.

- Be sure to repeat what you are hearing and how you imagine it can be implemented. Then ask if you heard correctly.

- Once you and your true self feel complete, thank your true self for its support and guidance, and return to your breathing process.

- When you are ready, slowly allow your eyes to open and focus back into the room where you find yourself.

- Write down what you heard. What did you learn? What insights did you gain?

Picking Up Someone Else's Frequency

Have you ever been around someone in great joy? Great pain? Someone in love? In depression? Perhaps you "knew" of their experience without them having to say a word.

Parents know how this works when their children are babies. The baby can be just fine when someone walks into the room and suddenly, the baby becomes distressed, upset, crying, etc. And as soon as that person leaves the room, the baby calms down again.

The inverse happens as well. The baby can be agitated or distressed when someone walks into the room and suddenly the baby is calm again.

What happens here? If you are a parent, you know these kinds of things take place, and the person who walked into the room did not have to do or say anything to change the experience of the baby.

Please consider playing the "what if" game here, no matter what your self-talk may be telling you. What if the baby has a "receiver" or "tuner" that recognizes the "frequency" the other person is broadcasting? What if the calm baby picks up the distressed frequency of the other person and responds with its own version of distress? Or, what if the distressed baby picks up the calm frequency of the other person and returns to its own state of calm or well-being?

Cognitive psychologists Ramsey M. Raafat, Nick Chater, and Chris Frith have written extensively on the phenomenon often referred to as herd psychology. Their research, published by the National Institutes of Health, suggests that humans can transmit "frequencies" associated with mental or emotional states that can be "picked up" by others and, in turn, change the mental or emotional state of others.

Have you ever found yourself wondering "where did that thought (or feeling) come from?" Maybe, just maybe, thoughts and emotions are frequencies or energies themselves and, as such, can be both transmitted as well as received.

During the COVID-19 pandemic in 2020, I worked with hundreds of parents via Zoom conferences worldwide, encouraging them to be "mindful" of what internal thoughts and fears they were "keeping inside" lest they disturb or upset the family. Many parents confirmed that their children would sometimes react in uncharacteristically agitated ways without anything seemingly taking place externally. Could it be that those children, much like the babies referenced above, were sensitive to the mental and emotional energies of their parents, or perhaps even larger groups (neighbors, etc.) and began reacting to those frequencies?

If you're up for a bit more on the physics side of invisible energy, let's consider something pretty ordinary—a piano. If you have ever been to a classical concert, you will have experienced the orchestra tuning up before they begin playing.

Typically, the concertmaster plays an A on their violin to which everyone else plays their A to make certain everyone is on the same pitch (frequency). Before doing so, the concertmaster would have tuned their instrument to the middle A key of the piano, which vibrates at 440 Hz. (Back in 1953, a worldwide agreement declared that middle A on the piano be forevermore tuned to exactly 440 Hz. This frequency became the standard ISO-16 reference for tuning all musical instruments based on the chromatic scale, the one most often used for music in the West.)

While knowing how orchestras tune up may not be terribly interesting, this next bit may be quite revelatory. If you were in a room full of pianos, and you were to strike the middle A key of any piano, *all the other middle A strings of all the other pianos would also begin vibrating.* Basic physics here—because those middle A strings are all constructed to vibrate at 440 Hz, any 440 Hz string will vibrate when that frequency is transmitted.

Humans have our own equivalent of middle A. That's why babies may react to the "frequency" of another being, why "herd psychology" works, and why you just might be able to "vibrate" in "harmony" with the "vibe" someone else is putting out.

In other words, maybe it is entirely real that we can pick up on the thoughts and feelings of others, even if we're not aware that we are doing so. My spiritual teacher, John-Roger, put it this way: *You're not responsible for the thoughts that come into your head, only to those that you hold onto.* Again, have you ever wondered "where did that (thought or feeling) come from?" (If this idea of connected energies intrigues you, then you may find listening to Dr. Jill Bolte Taylor, a prominent neuroscientist, describe having a stroke in real time. In the process of her stroke, she discovered her connection to the infinite. You can read more about her experience and discoveries in her fabulous book, *My Stroke of Insight,* or watch her TED talk by the same title.)

You might want to take a minute to check in with your true self, with your soul-talk, and listen to what it has to say about your current life experience. What would your true self have you focus on in your life? Are there "energetic" connections, lessons, or insights that it would have you notice and consider? *What if?*

Energy Follows Thought

Integrating focus with energy brings us to the notion that energy follows thought. You undoubtedly have experienced many versions of this simple fact. For example, have you ever been hungry, thought about one of your favorite foods, and then found saliva forming in your mouth? What's that all about? You didn't eat anything requiring saliva, and yet, there it is. You can apply this same experience to a range of other thoughts or fantasies that wind up with your body responding as though you were actually engaged in the physical act—I'll leave this to your imagination for further details.

Another example: Have you ever thought about engaging in an activity that you find scary? It could be anything from a trip to the dentist to confronting someone to meeting with your boss to ask for a raise. Pick anything that you find unsettling in some way.

As you begin thinking about that person or situation, you may find your self-talk adding a dose of negative input, reminding you of how these situations have gone in the past. As you persist in the thought, you may find your stomach or shoulders tensing up, maybe even to the point of upset or physical pain—and nothing was happening in the "real world."

Why? Because your body cannot tell the difference between a well-imagined thought and reality. As you persist in the thought, your body supplies the relevant experience or energy to match the thought. Again, that could include a wide range of experiences including saliva, sexual stimulation, or fear responses.

If you recognize that your own life experiences validate the premise, then you might want to consider taking dominion over your thought process, creating areas of focus that you would find rewarding, uplifting, or generally positive.

EXERCISE

Paper Clips and Visualization

Are you ready for another experiment? This one involves a paper clip and some thread. It works best with a larger paper clip, but any size can work. Take a piece of sewing thread about 18 to 24 inches in length and tie it to one end of the paper clip. Holding the loose end of the thread between your thumb and forefinger, let the paper clip hang unobstructed like a pendulum. If you like, you can also balance your elbow on a desk, table, or some other hard surface.

Now, with the paper clip hanging by the thread between your thumb and forefingers, simply imagine the paper clip swinging back and forth, from your left to your right and back again. Pretty soon, you will probably see the paper clip beginning to swing in the imagined direction. You can also try imagining it swinging out away from and back toward you. Once you get one of these going, imagine the paper clip changing direction, beginning to swing in a circle, clockwise or counterclockwise. It won't take too long before the paper clip begins to move in the imagined direction.

Feel free to play with this, imagining different swing paths, changes in direction, etc.

What's happening here?

I did this back in the early 1980s in Boston for a group of neurologists who were attending a management course. As most of the doctors found their paper clips swinging, one of them exclaimed rather loudly, "this is bullsh**t."

When I asked what made him say that, he stated rather emphatically that our thoughts were NOT making the paper clips swing; rather, it was minor movements in the hands or fingers that were amplified down the length of the thread and, thus, the paper clip was moving. All physical, nothing to do with our thoughts or imaginations.

To his surprise, I agreed—to a point. I asked if he had been trying to move his hand. He had not. I then asked if he could tell me which neuromuscular pathways were engaged to produce the movement. He could not.

My suggestion to him was to consider that by focusing on the outcome, his body took over producing the micro-movements required for the paper clip to move. His mind created the focus and his body cooperated because *energy follows thought.*

I also pointed to some research about sports figures who spent time "practicing" their sport mentally and the improved outcomes that could be observed in a variety of settings.

He was still unconvinced, so I asked him to think about someone dealing with paralysis. Is the paralysis caused by something in the muscular or skeletal system? No. It's caused by nerve signals no longer traveling below the level of spinal injury to the relevant muscles which in turn control movement. I asked the group to consider the possibility that one day they might be able to insert microscopic "wires" into the part of the brain associated with neuromuscular control and connect the wires directly to the muscles involved. Could they imagine that signals from the brain could be transmitted to the muscles and result in movement?

Today, there are all manner of experiments showing great promise in a field known as neuroprosthetics.

Excerpted from a *Washington Post* article published March 29, 2017:

> Bill Kochevar didn't feed himself for more than eight years, nor did he scratch his nose. He couldn't. A bicycle accident in 2006 left him nearly completely paralyzed from the shoulders down.
>
> Now, as outlined in research published Tuesday in the Lancet, Kochevar regained usage of his right hand with the help of an experimental technology called a neuroprosthetic. It essentially created a new connection between the brain and limb to replace the one that was broken.

For the first time in eight years, the 56-year-old Cleveland resident moved his arm simply by thinking about it. He drank a cup of coffee, munched on a pretzel and fed himself mashed potatoes.

"It was amazing," Kochevar said in a video published by Case Western Reserve University. "I thought about moving my arm, and it did. I could move it in and out, up and down."

"We have been able to take the electrical signals which represent his thoughts and use that to control stimulation of his arm and hand," said the study's lead author, Abidemi Bolu Ajiboye, assistant professor at Case Western Reserve University.

How about that paper clip?

CHAPTER 8

LEARNING TO SEE THE INVISIBLE

The intuitive mind is a sacred gift, and the rational mind is a faithful servant. We have created a society that honors the servant and has forgotten the gift.

—Albert Einstein

Damn, I Knew It.

Have you ever slapped yourself upside the head and exclaimed something like this? If you're like most people, you know what I'm talking about. We've all done something that didn't work out and in hindsight recognized that we had some kind of inner early warning signal that told us not to go there. Yet, we did it anyway.

Most of us have had the opposite experience as well. We did something, it worked out, and we wound up exclaiming, "I knew it!" This time, without the "Damn."

As it turns out, we all have the ability to "know" something without any apparent reason for knowing it.

What's the difference between knowing something that turns out great and knowing something that turns out badly?

Awareness. Simple awareness. Or more to the point, paying attention to our inner awareness.

There's a voice inside, often a big noisy voice, sometimes so subtle that it's hard to hear. But the voice is there, nonetheless.

You can call it annoying, or you can celebrate it.

Sometimes we pay attention, sometimes, not so much.

With practice, you may find that your inner awareness becomes more attuned to the messages emanating from your soul-talk. You may begin to recognize messages that slipped by you earlier but are now becoming increasingly clear.

What Are You Seeing That Is Not Yet Visible?

This subtle yet powerful question was put to me by Frances Hesselbein as we sat down together for the first time in 20 years. Frances was the CEO of The Leader to Leader Institute, formerly known as the Drucker Foundation for Nonprofit Management, and someone Peter Drucker once called the most effective executive in America.

Amongst her legendary accomplishments, she was awarded the Presidential Medal of Freedom for turning around the Girl Scouts of America and was the first woman appointed to chair The Study of Leadership at the United States Military Academy at West Point. Serving on many important boards of directors and having edited 27 books on business, Ms. Hesselbein was no starry-eyed lightweight wandering aimlessly through life.

In this one telling question, Frances reveals a key secret to leadership, be that leadership of an organization, your family, or your own life. In my experience, rather than being the exclusive ground of the leadership or visionary elite, seeing that which is not yet visible is, in fact, the ground of whom we truly are.

We each have access to information for which the body, mind, and emotions can be useful tools for bringing awareness and ideas into fruition—more commonly known as intuition. But to discover these new visions, we need to allow ourselves to look, to see, to imagine in new ways.

Soul-Centered Vision: Seeing with Spiritual Eyes

When Frances asked me what I was seeing that was not yet visible, I suddenly connected a host of dots that took me back another 35 years. It was 1978 and I was "blind as a bat," to use the vernacular. My glasses were so thick that without them I literally could not tell if a person were male or female from five feet away.

Someone had pointed me toward a then-experimental eye surgery known as radial keratotomy and a gifted surgeon, Dr. Ronald Jensen. The day before my first surgery, I was meeting with my spiritual teacher, John-Roger, when he said something jarring—as in awakening. "Russell, while the problem with your vision is now physical, the source isn't." When I asked him what he meant, he went on to say, "For years now you have been straining to see with your physical eyes that which can only be seen with your spiritual eyes."

Over the next several years, as J-R and I worked together facilitating Insight Seminars, he showed me a variety of ways of noticing deeper levels of awareness—inner vision, spiritual vision, soul-centered vision. In the process, he helped me attune to what I now call my soul-talk, a form of soul-guided inner dialogue revealing to me all manner of subtle awareness or knowledge, something we called "natural knowing."

Coupling soul-talk with my "spiritual eyes" has allowed me to discern numerous possibilities in life. I suggest that you can as well. It may require a leap of faith to pause, step beyond the self-limiting nature of your self-talk, and ask what you are noticing that is not yet visible, not yet audible. Slowing down long enough to ask these simple questions can be enormously revealing. I still need to remind myself that the information is available to me if I am available to the information. My version of slowing down is to sit quietly in a form of meditation, looking more deeply within, asking for those subtle insights to be revealed.

Intuition: Accessing Inner Guidance

If you are a business leader, you may already know the power of intuition in creating the future. Intuition and gut instinct are more commonly used terms for what I've been referring to as your soul-talk or soul-centered vision.

This may sound familiar by now—soul-talk and soul-centered vision are variations on the theme of intuition but with a bit more guidance on how to access the fabled world of intuition and gut instinct. Soul-talk encourages us to listen inwardly to that softer voice while soul-centered vision encourages us to "look" with our spiritual eyes.

In case this all sounds a bit too fluffy, here's what a few well-known business and science leaders have to say on the subject:

"Intuition is a very powerful thing, more powerful than intellect." —**Steve Jobs**

"I'm often wrong, but my batting record is good enough that I keep swinging every time the ball is thrown."—**Bill Gates** referring to his gut instinct in an interview with CNN in 2002 (Gates is also quoted as saying: "Often you have to rely on intuition.")

"I only do what my gut tells me to, I think it's smart to listen to other people's advice, but at the end of the day, you're the only one who can tell you what's right for you."—**Jennifer Lopez (J. Lo)**

"I rely far more on gut instinct than researching huge amounts of statistics."—**Richard Branson**

"The intellect has little to do on the road to discovery. There comes a leap in consciousness, call it intuition or what you will, the solution comes to you and you don't know how or why."—**Albert Einstein**

"Intuition becomes increasingly valuable in the new information society precisely because there is so much data."—**John Naisbitt**

"Intuition is seeing with the soul."—**Dean Koontz**

Intuition can show up in a variety of ways, ranging from a subtle sense (gut feeling, gut instinct, etc.) to a stronger, even compelling inner awareness or guidance. Sometimes, you might hear an inner dialogue. It can also show up in the sense Frances was pointing me toward—a kind of inner vision of something not quite visible. If you like, soul-talk, soul-centered vision, intuition, and gut instinct are interchangeable terms for the same process of inner knowing. The key point, which we will continue to explore, is that some aspect of who we are knows, as in *knows*, because it is connected to a deeper knowing through our true self, our soul.

Soul-centered vision can see past what is physically present and into that which is about to become visible. I'm pretty sure you have had some experiences wherein you saw something that was not yet visible that later came to pass. Have you ever heard or noticed something "for the first time" and exclaimed to yourself, "I knew that!" As in the past—at some earlier time you "knew that." And you really did. On one occasion, you may have seen it earlier but did nothing with it; on another occasion, perhaps you saw or sensed something earlier and acted on it.

If you recognize the notion of "I knew it," regardless of whether you *knew it and blew it* or sensed it and acted on it, you have had the experience of seeing life through the inner vision of what I call "soul-centered eyes." You have probably experienced both sides of this kind of awareness.

I'm suggesting that we've all "known that" beforehand, but perhaps denied what we were seeing or hearing, allowing it to remain hidden just below the level of the visible. Sometimes we see or hear something inwardly and our mind takes over in the form of that obnoxious inner critic wherein our self-talk tells us "That can't possibly be true," or "get a grip—you'll never be able to do that" or other forms of self-limitation. The only problem? What if you were seeing, hearing, or sensing something not yet visible? Was it tangible yet? Not so much. Real, nonetheless? Absolutely.

How did the iPhone come about? Or that computer you may be using to read this? Surely that device didn't magically appear and then get named the iPhone or MacBook. The visionaries of the world operate out of curiosity, creativity, and imagination; they come up with visions of mobile devices before anything has been constructed—they may start with nothing more profound than a vision of a need being fulfilled. That's how things work in my experience. Someone begins to see something not yet visible, often called the creative imagination or intuition, and then sets about doing the work necessary to discover what is required to translate an inner vision into an outer reality.

Another version of this kind of access to "invisible" possibility can be found in that old cliché, "necessity is the mother of invention." What on earth does that mean? How about using John F. Kennedy's challenge on May 25, 1961, when he said:

> We choose to go to the Moon . . . We choose to go to the Moon
> in this decade and do the other things, not because they are
> easy, but because they are hard; because that goal will serve
> to organize and measure the best of our energies and skills,
> because that challenge is one that we are willing to accept,
> one we are unwilling to postpone, and one we intend to win,
> and the others, too.

In many ways, Kennedy's moon challenge was a form of *energy follows thought*. He even referenced the idea when he said, "that goal will serve to organize and measure the best of our energies and skills."

Keep in mind that in 1961, the technology did not exist to accomplish this seemingly impossible feat. Many who teach people to accomplish major goals insist that one prerequisite to success requires focusing on the successful outcome, before focusing on the "how" to do it. When the reticular formation has guidance in the form of a clear goal or outcome, it begins scanning the environment for the "how" and "what" that will be necessary to succeed.

Success does not start with how we will do this, but with a clear, energetic focus on a desirable outcome.

The idea has been around us forever, perhaps most simply and elegantly stated by George Bernard Shaw and later paraphrased by Robert Kennedy: "Some people see things as they are and say why? I dream things that never were and say, why not?"

If you can dream something that is not yet visible, you just may be able to do something about translating the dream into reality. However, creating something in the real world takes a lot more than simply having a vision or a dream. You need to test the range of what appears to be possible given your circumstances, conditions, and a host of practical questions.

Part of the challenge is that seeing through soul-centered eyes or listening to your soul-talk rarely comes complete with an operating manual. You must be willing to test what you are seeing or hearing inwardly and then risk doing the work to transform it into something real.

Doing the hard work of testing, refining, starting over, etc., is enough for most people to give up before they even start. Edison went through over 1,000 combinations of gas and filament before his vision of a lightbulb turned out to be real and sustainable. Good thing his self-talk had not been programmed to notice obstacles, limitations, and flaws, otherwise he may have heard its loud voice reminding him of all his previous failures: "What makes you think you can make this next one work?"

So now we have a grand challenge: Are we seeing something which is not yet visible or are we simply in the realm of self-delusion? If you focus on the former, you will marshal your inner resources and begin to imagine how to bring the vision into existence. If you choose the latter, your self-talk will shut you down so quickly that there won't be anything to do. How do you know the difference?

That's a great question. How do you go about discerning between inspiration and illusion, between pure fantasy and seeing or perceiving that which is not yet visible? For me, the process is one of staying ever vigilant, ever mindful, paying attention to what I see inwardly and what shows up in the "real" world. My process of vigilant mindfulness is a combination of daily meditation and checking things out along the way in "the real world." If I am truly seeing something not yet visible, the vision will persist through multiple meditation sessions, augmented by discussions with others, brainstorming, and other approaches to creative development.

CHAPTER 9

THE UNIVERSE REWARDS ACTION, NOT THOUGHT

*When something vibrates, the electrons of the entire universe reso-
nate with it. Everything is connected. The greatest tragedy
of human existence is the illusion of separateness.*

—Albert Einstein

Imagine for a moment that there is something out there called "the
universe" and that it holds the ability to produce whatever you
might like in your life, be it on the Symbols side or the Experience
side. With all the "I-wish-I-had" thoughts being sent, how is "the
universe" going to respond?

The theory here is that *the universe rewards action, not thought.*
It's probably obvious that we need to start with a thought or awareness of what's possible before we can take action. That thought could
be of the mundane variety or divinely inspired. Rarely does anything
substantial show up in the real world without a guiding thought or
idea.

However, the thought or inspiration alone is insufficient without acting toward the goal or desired outcome. Consider the Edison
example—he had to think up the hundreds of filament and gas combinations, and he then had to put them together and test them.
That's the action part of the equation. With each unsuccessful combination, he learned more, perhaps clarified some part of the idea,
and then took the next step.

Directionally Correct, Not Perfectionally Correct

How many times have you come up short in your life because you couldn't come up with a "perfect" answer or solution? Have you ever experienced your self-talk showing up just as you got the least bit excited about a new possibility or choice with "helpful" admonitions along the lines of "that will never work," or "who are you kidding" or simply reminding you of all the times you "failed" in the past? In a way, your self-talk is trying to do you a favor, to protect you from disappointment. At the same time, it is also "protecting" you from success.

In Edison's case, he managed to keep his internal vision and focus on the outcome, not on the intermediate "missteps" along the way. While many of the combinations of gas and filament "failed" to produce the desired result, he was, nonetheless, "directionally correct"—his actions and combinations were simply steps along the way to the successful outcome. He just didn't know how many steps it was going to take to complete his "thousand-mile journey."

Lao Tzu and the Journey of a Thousand Miles

The Chinese philosopher, Lao Tzu, provided us a wonderful gift with his simple reminder that "A journey of a thousand miles begins with a single step." Many other traditions have their versions of this simple truth. The obvious part of this wisdom reduces to the simple fact that we can't get anywhere if we don't start.

The not-so-obvious aspect of this bit of enlightenment lies in the implication that we can know in advance how many steps it will take to complete the thousand-mile journey. If you're a numbers person, like an accountant or engineer, you may be tempted to measure your average stride, divide that into 1,000 miles, and figure out how many steps it will take to complete the journey.

While this measurement approach may seem anywhere from ridiculous to practical, it falls apart in reality. That thousand-mile journey may include unexpected detours (the bridge was out), interesting or attractive stops along the way, or any number of unanticipated "extra" steps.

If you're committed to the "finish line," to the outcome, you will take as many steps as it takes to get there. If your self-talk tracks your steps, once you have taken the forecasted number, it may tell you "That's enough" and (dis)encourage you to quit.

"Enough already" is a phrase all of us have heard, if not muttered ourselves. However, if we haven't arrived at the destination, then clearly it wasn't enough. Paraphrasing my spiritual teacher: "Don't worry about deciding how much is enough; enough will declare itself when it truly is enough."

Edison was committed to the lightbulb, not to how many steps or combinations were required along the way.

Once you have committed to start working in the direction of your desired outcome, you are likely to be met by a supporting force helping you get there.

Whether you believe in "the universe" or not is pretty much irrelevant. There well may be some big source out there waiting for you to get clear and move on your clarity. Even if there isn't, your true self is paying attention and will supply the energy necessary (energy follows thought) as long as you demonstrate real commitment by taking action toward your desired outcome.

Have you ever told yourself that you were going to change something (eat more healthily, exercise regularly, save money, etc.) and haven't followed through? When we tell ourselves through our thoughts, imaginations, or daydreams that something is important, there's a part of us, our self-talk, who is listening, one who may have heard it so many times before but also noticed the lack of follow-through. What happens when we tell ourselves something is important and then do not follow through? Which do you think counts more? What we tell ourselves or what we act upon?

How does that person inside of you know when you mean it or not? It could be as simple as whether you act on your thoughts or not. We all know the truth of *actions speak louder than words.*

Continuing to put this all together, let's look a bit more closely at something we said earlier about "energy follows thought." You may recall that we are talking about the role of imagination and how well-constructed thoughts can help produce the energy necessary to bring those thoughts to fruition.

Why Words Matter: Definition vs. Direction

It's probably obvious that I like to work with words in terms of what they mean energetically. Many people are concerned about definitions of words, which I understand and play with also. To "define" a word is to put boundaries around it, declaring "it is this, and not that." Precise definitions can be quite helpful in some situations and not so much in others.

I tend to be more interested in what words mean in terms of direction, how they help us move energy. Consider for a moment that the reason words came about in the first place was to help us move energy from one place to another. Whether it was about gathering food (a form of energy needed to survive), looking for a friend or companion, or seeking safety, words came about to help us both individually as well as collectively.

For example, a glass is different from a mug to be sure. However, if someone were thirsty and said they needed a glass of water and all you had was a mug, would you tell them you couldn't help them because you didn't have a glass? Of course not! You would immediately understand the energetic need and fulfill the request regardless of the definition of the vessel holding the water. Said differently, the purpose or intent of our words is often more important than the sometimes narrow boundaries or definitions of the actual words we use.

Imagination and Visualization: Images Requiring Action

Merriam-Webster defines imagine as "to form a mental image of (something not present)" and imagination as "the act or power of forming a mental image of something not present to the senses or never before wholly perceived in reality." To me, this suggests that *seeing that which is not yet visible* is pretty much universally known and has been for a long time. After all, it's even in the dictionary!

If we further deconstruct the word *imagination*, we find additional clues as to how this works. The first key word making up the words *imagine* and *imagination* is "image." According to Merriam-Webster, an image is *a mental picture or impression of something.* To imagine something then is to hold a mental picture of something not yet present. The suffix, *ation*, comes from the Latin root word for action, meaning *do.* Simply stated then, imagination is the process of holding a mental image of something not yet present and then doing something about it. In other words, imagination means *to image in and act it out.*

It can be helpful to think of imagination as a simple construct for *energy follows thought* with the additional requirement of *acting on that energy.* Thought enables or enlivens the energy necessary to bring about the object of our thoughts, and we still need to use that energy in an active, engaging way.

The Power of Thought—Is It Thought or Belief?

Many of us have built our lives on beliefs and ideas we have accepted from others as truth. One such notion is the power and importance of thought.

As noted earlier, the body can't distinguish between a well-imagined thought and reality. Again, you can fantasize about eating a favorite food and find saliva in your mouth to help digest what you haven't consumed. So, if the body feels something, does that make it true, or at least present? Of course not.

However, if you persist in a thought long enough, you may find yourself generating the energy or enthusiasm to get up and do something about it. In the simplest form, you could persist in the thought about eating that particularly yummy food and find yourself in search of some. I know I have done that sitting at home, thinking about the ice cream I didn't have, and found myself driving to the store to buy some.

If your self-talk persists in repeating old stories or beliefs, much like the sidebar on the next page on my experience growing up with a Depression-era mom and dad, then you may find yourself directing energy into something not useful, perhaps not even true.

Energy follows thought works in many ways, some with positive outcomes, some not so much. Sometimes, we act on the energy that follows our thoughts, but not always. I know I have found myself daydreaming about something, getting all hot and bothered inside about it, and still wound up doing nothing.

Here we have the makings of an interesting conundrum: *energy follows thought* can work for you or against you depending on how you work it inside of yourself. Imagination, visualization, and affirmations can produce the energy and impetus to take positive action toward your ideal outcomes.

However, if you take the more passive daydreaming route, your self-talk may tell you that "all this positive thinking/imagination stuff is just fantasy." And, it will have proof: the absence of anything to show for all the daydreaming is the "proof" that imagination and visualization just don't work. In this case, the lack of energy follows negative or limiting thought.

All this begs the question: What is the difference between daydreaming and the process of imagination and visualization? The occasional daydream rarely produces sufficient energy to get up and go, especially if the self-talk is there reminding us that this stuff never works for us.

Persisting in the positive imagery of a successful outcome makes it much more likely to generate the energy or motivation (motive for action) required to bring about the desired change or outcome.

Can You Use Daydreaming for a Positive Outcome?

My daydreams might be nice, but daydreaming about a new car seldom produces a new car. However, dreaming about the new car

HOW CONFLICTING BELIEFS HAVE LIMITED ME

Let me take you into a bit of how I grew up to illustrate one aspect of the power of beliefs, how they sometimes get created, and how an early belief can continue to influence choices for years to come.

My parents were born and raised in Depression-era Iowa, my mom in a small town of 400, and my dad on a family farm. They didn't have much back then.

Growing up, we didn't have much in the way of life's luxuries either, but I was happy. As I was about to start first grade, I remember my mom taking me to the local JCPenney store to get my school clothes. On the way to the store, Mom kept saying things about how tough it had been for her as a little girl from a family without much money and how embarrassed she was going to school in hand-me-downs while all the "rich" kids had new clothes. Her children were not about to suffer that indignity.

And that's when it began—the installation of a belief about life. The way I remember it, she would say the following, almost like a mantra or rosary: *"We may not have much, but we'll always have clothes on our backs, shoes on our feet, and food on the table."* She learned this mantra herself growing up in the Great Depression with a father who repeated it to her regularly.

This was a theme that repeated through many circumstances, ranging from school clothes to all kinds of life's basics. I'll spare you the details, but my family went bankrupt. Three times! Bankruptcy was just another event to me, but traumatic to my mom and dad.

And so it was as I grew up. For 18 years, clothes on the back, shoes on the feet, and food on the table were seemingly constant refrains.

As far as I was concerned, life was good, and the simple things were more than fine. I certainly didn't lack anything that I noticed. I'm sure others were more well off, and I can remember visiting some of their homes, but I just never put it together as us being less well off. Their homes looked like their homes, and ours looked like ours and that was about all there was to it.

Fast forward to my early 30s. I had created Insight Seminars, teaching others about improving their quality of life. One evening, as I was standing on stage in front of 200 people, trying to get a point across about the limiting nature of beliefs, I suddenly became aware of the "clothes on the back, shoes on the feet, and food on the table" thing.

At the time, I was earning what I thought was a very modest yet comfortable salary. I shared a two-bedroom apartment with a roommate, and my bank account was just big enough to be in a real bank, instead of a piggy bank.

And suddenly, there on the stage, I became aware of some stunning insights into myself and how I had been living my life. While I did not have much in the way of material world possessions, I did have "clothes on the back, shoes on the feet, and food on the table." Did I ever!

I had a great wardrobe—beautiful suits, fine shirts, Italian shoes. I often ate in restaurants, enjoying fine dining and great wine.

And, while I "didn't have much, I did have clothes on the back, shoes on the feet, and food on the table."

Oh my! It suddenly began to dawn on me that beliefs about life that had begun developing as a child were now running my day-to-day choices. Unconscious as they might have been, there they were in plain view for me to see now.

It seemed like every time I earned a bit more money, and began to build my bank account, I found another suit, pair of shoes, or fine bottle of wine that I just had to have. I went home that night, got out a pencil and pad, and began to list all the "stuff" that I had accumulated in my modest little apartment.

Turns out I had a small fortune in clothes and shoes alone. My bank account hadn't ever hit the $5,000 mark while my "clothes on the back and shoes on feet" account was overflowing.

Hmmm. A belief I held about what it means to be "one of us" (a Bishop) had led to a whole set of choices about how to live that had resulted in a huge imbalance on where my money went. And I hadn't even noticed!

(or job or relationship or just about anything else for that matter) directs a lot of energy toward the object of your desire. As you continue to put even more energy into the dream, your reticular system will begin discovering an array of options or choices to bring the dream into reality.

If you have ever daydreamed about a new (car, house, item of clothing, etc.) you may have also found that they seem to "suddenly appear" all over the place. If you keep an image in your mind about that new car, you may find that you begin noticing them frequently. It's not that they suddenly appeared out of nowhere; rather, your reticular system was now programmed to notice them whereas before, they were just background. And notice them it did.

The more we revisit the dream, the more we may begin to entertain options for bringing the dream into reality. Sometimes, the choice is as obvious as going to the car dealership where they sell those kinds of cars and buying one. This one is easy if you already have the finances to buy one. Another, less obvious choice, is to enter a raffle where that kind of car is being raffled off (can't win if you don't enter kind of thinking). Another choice is to simply tell as many people as you can about your ideal outcome, and maybe someone will present you with a gift (not the most common occurrence, but it does happen!)

For most of us, finding a way to buy the car will be the most obvious and workable solution. But what happens if you don't have the wherewithal to buy that car? You may have already noticed that if you keep your focus on something you would like, you begin to make subtle changes in your habits that make buying the car more likely. It can be as simple as cutting out some of your spending, saving a bit here and there, and building up enough for that down payment. Your self-talk may tell you that this approach is just another unworkable fantasy, persuading you to "give up the dream" before even starting. However, if you persist in the imagination and visualization, you may find those subtle changes become easy, even natural.

As much as you can think or dream about what you might want in your life, as much as you can be clear in your vision and support that vision by affirmations, as much as you can stay focused and positive in your mind, you probably won't wind up with a positive result until you get actively involved in producing what you want.

That's because *the universe rewards action, not thought.*

This gets tricky because there are so many different ways of creating out there.

Some will need to get out there and work their tails off to produce the income to buy the car. Others will just dip into their sizeable bank accounts. Still others will find that letting others know of their intention somehow attracts to them the means to produce the object of their desire.

There are many ways to produce the outcome in the physical world. Very rarely, though, does someone create a clear vision, support that vision with positive thoughts and affirmations, and have the car show up in their living room while they are busy thinking about it and visualizing the good outcome.

The key is active participation.

Affirmations—the Role of Positive Thinking

Affirmations can help support active participation. Much like the word *imagination, affirmation* contains a few clues as to its workability. Merriam-Webster tells us that to affirm means "to show or express a strong belief in or dedication to (something, such as an important idea)." Affirmation then means to express a strong belief or dedication to an idea *and then act on it.*

Affirmations are positive statements reinforcing the desired outcome (man on the moon by the end of the decade) which help keep the reticular formation and your creative process focused. They help immeasurably with the notion of *energy follows thought.* The more expansive your vision and affirmation, the more you hold the positive thought and focus on your desired outcome, the more you may experience the enlivening of your energy to bring about the new circumstance.

As your inner vision and soul-talk perceive a new possibility (consider your Wheel for a moment and how you would like it to change for the better) and your enthusiasm builds, your self-talk may show up again, reminding you of all the times in the past that you failed, came up short, or just gave up. If, however, you persist in the positive focus and begin taking those micro-steps, eventually, your self-talk will get on board.

Changing behavior along with the accompanying mindset requires a combination of patience, persistence, and perseverance. Researchers, psychologists, and behavioral change experts suggest that it can take anywhere from 21 days to 254 days to build a new habit or focus. My own experience suggests that somewhere around 33 consecutive days can build up the energy, focus, and discipline necessary to facilitate a desired change.

Following is a personal example of something I experienced after I had finished graduate school and was busy avoiding taking any meaningful steps to improve my life and advance my career. I still had a goodly amount of self-doubt, and my self-talk was right there to remind me that other people were better than me in any number of ways, so why bother. I was discovering that just because someone else is better than me doesn't mean that I can't improve or succeed if I can learn to keep my focus on the positive outcome I would most prefer.

Maintaining a Positive Focus

I first encountered the power of focusing on the desired outcome supported by a positive affirmation when I took a positive thinking course called Mind Dynamics. The class was facilitated by a fabulous young man who later became a mentor of mine, Randy Revell.

As Randy facilitated this class of 30 people, I was struck by how energetic, confident, and capable he seemed in front of the room. To me, 30 people seemed like a huge crowd. I had participated in and led groups of 10 to 12, and the idea of working with 30 people seemed impossible.

On the third day of the course, Randy asked us to choose an area of life where we would like to experience improvement. I chose to focus on my career. The idea of facilitating "large groups" of people seemed both attractive and impossible at the same time. Attractive because I was fully committed to helping people after my tear gas experience at Berkeley; impossible because I just didn't have the self-confidence to imagine standing in front of such a "large" group.

Randy thought this was a "perfect" area for me. He asked me to close my eyes and imagine standing in front of a large group of people—what did I see? what did I look like standing in front of the group? He asked me to imagine people coming up to me and thank-ing me for my assistance, telling me that I had been helpful, that their lives were now better than before. He also asked me to imagine how I would feel seeing all those people, hearing all the good things they had to say.

Once I had the images in place, he then asked me to create an affirmation, a simple positive, present-tense statement about what I was imagining. Here's what I came up with: *I am strong, confident and in control of my life, doing what I want to do, when I want to do it.*

This affirmation would not win any affirmation prizes. However, it worked for me because, at that point in my life, I did not experience myself as "strong, confident, or in control of my life." Seeing myself standing in front of all those people and hearing all those positive comments seemed perfectly aligned with the affirmation I had created.

Randy then had me close my eyes again, imagining that I was watching this scene unfold on something like a TV or movie screen, all the while seeing the affirmation scrolling across the bottom of the screen.

Once I had this combination down, he then told me to practice this imagination and affirmation twice a day, once in the morning immediately upon waking up and *before* getting out of bed, and again in the evening while lying in bed right before falling asleep.

Randy suggested that practicing this routine for 30 consecutive days would assist in changing my inner images or beliefs about myself, which would then lead to changes in the "real world." In today's language and knowledge, he was assisting me to grow and reorganize my neural pathways, building new neural connections in support of my desired change.

I began this process in early June and maintained the discipline every day for several weeks. By the end of the summer, I had been hired by the Mind Dynamics company and was soon running these "large" classes.

Of course, it took a bit more than simply imagining and affirming the change for something tangible to take place. As noted earlier, positive thinking and positive focus establish the image, and it still requires positive action to bring about the change. In this instance, after I had been practicing the discipline of these daily visualizations and affirmations for a month or so, I contacted Randy and began asking how I could become a facilitator myself.

It took some moxie to venture out of my then familiar university comfort zone and risk asking for what I wanted. However, the daily visualization practice helped me build a "new familiar" accompanied by a growing inner sense of capability and courage. In my language of today, I would say that I learned to let my soul-talk lead and, in the process, began re-educating my self-talk in the direction of my preferred life path.

Can You Produce Energy by Expending Energy?

It may be a bit of a stretch to consider how this might be applicable, but please do follow along with the next set of questions—nothing to do or believe, just follow along and notice if anything resonates for you.

Have you ever exercised? Ever? Think about a time when you got the cardiovascular system going—perhaps a good run or jog, or some kind of aerobic exercise. Once you finished and your heart and respiration rate returned to normal, did you feel like you had more or less energy?

Most people will say that after exercising, they *feel* more energized, not less. This is one of those experiences where it's both true and false. While exercising, you were burning calories; therefore, from a measurement point of view, you must have less energy than you started with—after all, you just got through burning calories! However, your body more than likely felt more energized as a result of the exercise.

Why? Because the human body was designed to produce energy by expending energy. When you start to exercise and your heart rate rises, you begin to draw on the energy in your bloodstream—glucose or blood sugar. As you draw down the supply of blood sugar and continue to exercise, the body begins to pull the energy it needs from the glycogen stored in your muscles and liver, turning it into glucose or blood sugar.

Once you get this little energy engine working inside your body and finish exercising, the body continues to turn glycogen into glucose for a short time which, in turn, provides you with the experience of feeling better, more energetic.

While not exactly the same, it is an example of how the *universe rewards action, not thought.* You can think about exercising and nothing much will change. However, once you get up and get going, you will find you have more energy to continue.

Taking action, just about any action, will begin to produce some kind of result or experience. As you continue developing your awareness skills, you will likely begin to notice whether the action is moving you in the desired direction or not. The more you notice whether you are "on course" or "off course," the more you will discover additional clarity about the way forward and choices you can make.

Even if you take the "wrong" path, you can develop additional insights, awareness, or other forms of inner knowledge, allowing you to notice a choice, an avenue, a way forward that you may not have previously perceived. Your self-talk may regard those "wrong" path choices as mistakes, while your true self, your soul-talk, may instead regard them as learning opportunities. I have found that those wrong turns can lead to something beautiful that I might never have discovered save for the "wrong" turn.

Sometimes the reward was additional information about how to produce whatever I was seeking. Frequently the reward has been greater clarity about what I would truly prefer over what I had been seeking.

The key points are that to produce more of what we truly want in our life, we need (a) clarity about what we want and (b) why we want it in the first place and (c) to become actively engaged in producing it. Hence, *energy follows thought* and *the universe rewards action, not thought.*

EXERCISE

Creating Positive Change

You might consider creating your version of a positive change supported by positive visualizations and affirmations. Pick an area of your Wheel where you would like to experience a significant shift. Create an image of yourself in the new state—what would you see? What would others see? How would you feel? How would others feel about your change? Then come up with a positive statement that supports the desired change.

Here are some "starter" affirmations you might want to tinker with and come up with something that works for you.

- My seemingly impossible good is happening now.

- Every day, in every way, I am getting better and better (from Émile Coué).

- I am experiencing miracles as my seemingly impossible good is happening now.

- Abundance and prosperity manifest in perfect timing now for the highest good.

- God's love and energy manifest perfectly in every form and event in my life.

- I am living a life of grace, ease, and profound well-being.

- I contribute enormous value and people love working with me.

CHAPTER 10

WHEN GOALS AND BELIEFS COLLIDE

*We only see what we want to see; we only hear
what we want to hear. Our belief system is just like a mirror
that only shows us what we believe.*

—Don Miguel Ruiz

Have you ever noticed that even though you might be clear about what you want in life, you can still run into unanticipated conflicts or roadblocks? While it could be that you weren't all that clear in the first place, often, the issue may be that you held conflicting goals, beliefs, or intentions.

Even as your soul-talk may be pointing you toward a very uplifting change, encouraging you to step out in a new direction, your self-talk may be somewhere between hesitant and fearful, offering a range of cautionary thoughts or beliefs. Common admonitions include, "Who are you kidding? We don't deserve that kind of (success, goal, life, etc.)." Another familiar refrain, "these things never work out for us," or "we're not the kind of people who can achieve this kind of life."

Perhaps even more common is the experience of holding conflicting goals or desires. A simple one could be around losing weight and still wanting to eat ice cream every evening. Perhaps you want to build up your savings or investment account but keep bumping up against that new, bright shiny object that you just must have. For me, "clothes on the back, shoes on the feet, etc." was one of those.

Perhaps like me, you may find your self-talk telling you that "it's OK, just this once." Of course, giving in to "just this once" can easily lead to another "just this time" around the next corner.

How Beliefs Create Poverty

There are many beliefs we could examine that could hinder your ability to create your Wheel and the experiences you would most prefer in life. As we dig a bit deeper into this subject, I'm going to use beliefs about money as a focal point. I could have picked any number of subjects, but money seems to get people excited, exasperated, or otherwise engaged.

As we go through this exploration, notice how often your self-talk shows up, either confirming or arguing with various points. It's important to keep in mind that while your self-talk has your best interests in mind, it also has a vested interest in being right and in defending the choices you may have made that got you where you are in your life so far. Rather than blaming the self-talk, the goal is to notice what may be in the way and then provide a bit of self-education.

Here's a starter set of questions to get us moving.

- What beliefs do you hold about money?

- What is OK about money?

- What is not OK about money?

- What kinds of things have you heard about money from other people?

If any of the following commonly held beliefs sound familiar, they may play a role in limiting your ability to produce or hold onto money:

- Money can't buy me love (or happiness).

- It takes money to make money.

- Poor is pure (spiritual).

- I'm not worthy.

- Money is the root of all evil.

- If I had it, how would I know who my real friends are (vs. those who are just after my money)?

- Easy come, easy go.

- It takes hard work over a long time to make money.

- We're not the kind of people who will ever have money.

- Money is made on the backs of the poor.

- Champagne tastes and a beer budget.

- Money is dirty (filthy rich).

- Money will only burn a hole in my pocket.

- Too rich for my blood.

- The best things in life are free.

- It is easier for a camel to pass through the eye of a needle than it is for a rich man to enter the kingdom of heaven.

Does this list seem familiar? You might have others to add that I missed. So, let's think about this list of beliefs in light of our earlier discussion about Symbols vs. Experience.

When I work with groups, I typically ask for a show of hands—who would like more money than they currently have? Most hands go up. Does yours? No big deal either way, just sort of a benchmark for the rest of the discussion.

The "what if" part of this conversation goes something like: "What if you could have just about anything you wanted and the only limiting variables were your inner beliefs?"

If that were true, then each of us could create darn near anything. Again, do you recognize any from the list of beliefs above that might hold a person back from having more money?

If you believe that "the best things in life are free," why would you need money? Don't get me wrong here—I'm not arguing with the truth or lack of truth in this or any other of these statements. It's just a question of what beliefs you hold and how they might impact your behavior or even your perception of available choices.

If you subscribe to the notion that money is made on the backs of other people's efforts, and you don't feel particularly good about "exploiting" others, then you might find it hard to make money.

If "it takes money to make money," and you don't have much to start with, then how can you ever make anything? Of course, it doesn't say that you need a lot of money to make money—just that you need some to start. How about those people who start with very little and accumulate lots? Or those who start with a lot and lose it?

It may be worth exploring how many different and possibly conflicting beliefs, goals, or intentions you might happen to hold at any one time.

How Beliefs Create Conflicting Outcomes

Beliefs are like vectors pointing in different directions. In physics, a vector is a quantity that has both magnitude and direction. In overly simplistic terms, a vector is a line indicating a force moving in a direction with the length of the line proportional to the amount

WHAT DOES EYE OF THE NEEDLE MEAN?

The "eye of the needle" story is a great example of how beliefs sometimes become ingrained from a misunderstanding of something small, yet critical.

The phrase "eye of a needle" is often used as a metaphor for a very narrow opening throughout various religious scriptures including the Talmud, the New Testament, and the Qur'an. New Testament passages in Matthew, Mark, and Luke about the camel and "eye of the needle" have been said to refer to a smaller gate (the eye) within a larger gate (The Needle Gate) into Jerusalem.

Many gates into ancient walled cities in the Middle East had large gates that would be closed at night to prevent marauders from charging in on horse or camelback and raining havoc. However, sometimes a caravan of the good guys would arrive at night, and they needed to be allowed entrance. Rather than risk opening the main gate, a smaller gate-within-a-gate, the so-called eye, could be opened.

A camel could not pass through the smaller gate unless it was stooped and had its baggage removed. The metaphor refers to the camel in two ways: a camel is not attached to the possessions it carries while the rich are often very attached. The camel needed to stoop or even get on its knees to enter through the "eye." Many rich are not that willing to "bow" or humble themselves. Hence, it is easier for the camel . . .

Remember earlier when I mentioned that I grew up in a Presbyterian family? I recall this passage about the camel and needle frequently being read just before the collection plate was passed. The not-so-subtle message for me went something like, *whoa, that's a very tiny hole—no way am I going to be rich!*

of force moving in that direction. For our purposes, you can think of goals, self-images, and beliefs as vectors. Some goals, self-images, and beliefs are stronger than others.

You may recall the principle of vector addition from your school days; if not, here's a simple graphic indicating different beliefs, while the diagonal arrow represents what shows up when the conflicting beliefs are left unchecked.

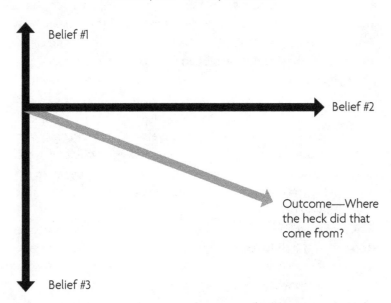

GOAL, SELF-IMAGE, OR BELIEF

Belief #1

Belief #2

Outcome—Where the heck did that come from?

Belief #3

Imagine holding a handful of these at the same time: money is the root of evil (you won't catch me being evil), the camel and needle story (hey, I want to be spiritual), takes money to make money (and I have none), and the best things in life are free. Holding any combination of these could make it difficult to make or have money.

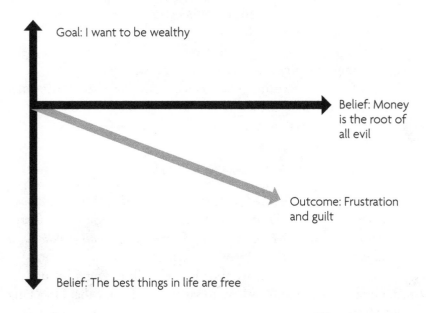

SELF-IMAGE: I'M SPIRITUAL

Goal: I want to be wealthy

Belief: Money is the root of all evil

Outcome: Frustration and guilt

Belief: The best things in life are free

What if: even though some part of you may want more money, if you hold other conflicting beliefs, self-concepts, or intentions, you may wind up blocking your ability to even perceive, let alone make choices that could lead to an improved monetary condition? My story about "clothes on the back, shoes on the feet, food on the table" is an example of how simple and subtle this process can be. In my case, while I wanted to build up a savings account, I kept finding shoes, clothes, and food I "just had to have—at least just this once."

Now, I'm not saying you should be looking to have more money. As already noted, my experience suggests that getting clear on the experiences you would prefer is far more important than focusing on the symbols side of the equation.

However, if you are going to live in this physical world, you may find it useful to have a bit more of the material world as you go about producing the experiences you truly seek. Hence, it might make sense to examine your inner beliefs from the point of view of possible conflict or self-sabotage.

(If you find this section interesting and would like to experience it more deeply, you may want to consider participating in an Insight Seminar: www.insightseminars.org. Many of these principles are part of the Insight programs I designed and are presented in a directly experiential manner.)

The Role of Self-Doubt

Have you ever considered a change of some magnitude or consequence, imagined what it might be like, and then found self-doubt entering your mind? *Can I do this? What might go wrong? Who am I kidding? I've never accomplished anything like this before.*

Even as I write this, I notice my self-talk raising a bit of self-doubt about what I might have to say, reminding me that I'm a long way from having consistently demonstrated these principles in my own life, let alone having mastered them.

Indeed, self-doubt and lack of confidence have been my companions since early childhood. I don't recall exactly when I moved from a confident and precocious little boy into the more shy and unconfident person I thought I was later in life.

Perhaps it began when my mother teased me about being small, often referring to me as "possible," as in I might possibly be good at something. Perhaps it began when I drew a profile of a Sioux Indian chief in the sixth grade. It was remarkably good, evidencing an ability none thought I possessed—so much so that my teacher told me there was no way I could have drawn it myself. Exit my foray into art.

Couple this sixth-grade experience with a combination of others, and somewhere along the line, I lost sight of my potential, of who I truly am. Over time, I began to doubt that I had much to offer, let alone much to hope for out of life.

Some contradictory lessons stand out in my mind, lessons I first learned as family sayings, almost family mottoes. There were others in addition to "We won't have much, but we will always have food on the table, clothes on our backs, and shoes on our feet." Among them, "Can't died in the poor house because he couldn't" juxtaposed with "You can be anything you want." (You may have to pause a moment and imagine "Can't" as the first name of a person, and then it will likely become clear.) "Don't get your hopes up—nothing good happens to the Bishops." And many more.

I have learned to call these "conflicting beliefs." Conflicting beliefs can lead my mind and self-talk in different directions at the same time, often resulting in a form of paralysis of action. If one part of me believes it can be anything it wants, then I may tend to dream big dreams. If another part of me believes it is hopeless because nothing good happens to people like us, then I won't put much effort into making those dreams come true.

"He's such a dreamer." Is that a pejorative phrase or a compliment? I guess that depends on what beliefs or self-images a person chooses to accept.

Chooses to accept? Now there's a key concept. As you will see in the next chapter, choice plays an increasingly important role on the road to *Becoming More of Who You Truly Are*. For the moment, I will simply pose a hypothetical question: What if everything we experience in life is a result of a choice or choices we have made or avoided making, consciously or unconsciously? Much like Mitchell didn't choose to be hit by the laundry van or become paralyzed in the plane crash, he did choose how he responded to what happened.

To make this more personal, and therefore more powerful, what if everything you experience in your life is a function of choices you have made? Again, not necessarily the circumstances, but how you have chosen to respond to those circumstances.

What if that were true? If that were true, then you and I would be incredibly powerful creators. If it all comes down to us and to the choices we make, then it would hold that we could create just about anything we want in life. What if that were true?

What if it is not true? What if life and our life experiences aren't just up to us and to the choices that we make? What if it's true some of the time and not others? Well, if it's not true, if life and experience in life just happen to us, outside of our ability to choose or influence, then that's just the way it is and it probably won't cost too much to explore the "what if" theory about choice.

But what if it is true that life and our life experiences are a function of our choices and our choices alone? If that were true, wouldn't it make sense to find out how?

Now, don't get me wrong here. There are holes in this "logic" big enough to cause real angst in a true philosopher, let alone a true pragmatist.

However, I am proposing that if you "play along" with the notion of "what if," that just possibly each of us is the author of our own experience, the creator of our own life. What if the key to life success is our ability to recognize and make choices? If so, then each of us might discover unforeseen capabilities to transform our experience of life into something truly magical.

How to Use Your Thoughts to Create What You Want

Let's return to the Wheel of Life and the Symbols vs. Experience exercises for a moment.

Pull out your Wheel and notice what it looks like in its current state. Pick an area where you would like to experience improvement.

As you contemplate the area for improvement, notice what your self-talk has to say about that area. Perhaps it might be something like one of these internal comments:

- *How many times have I tried to (lose weight, get fit, save money)?*

- *It takes too much work/effort to improve.*

- *People like me never seem to get ahead.*

- *They'd never hire (people like) me for that kind of job.*

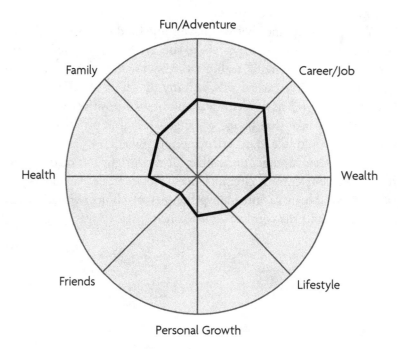

Fill in your responses. By holding thoughts like those, what kind of energy seems to follow? Probably not very motivating. They do produce energy, however, just not the kind that will help you get up off your dreams and do something, much less sustain the effort over time. If you keep up that kind of inner dialogue, how likely is it that you will put much energy into improving?

Take a moment right now and return to some form of a quick meditation or inner process: What would your soul-talk, your true self, encourage you to think, to tell yourself, or do? Remember to write down what you hear.

Let's look at the other side of this equation. Pick an area where you are experiencing the most success or fulfillment. Assuming you have an area above the 50% mark in terms of fulfillment, what kind of inner dialogue goes on there?

You will likely find that you have some kind of positive self-image or self-talk in those areas where you are doing reasonably well. Perhaps, something like: "Yeah, that's easy for me," "Of course, I'm good at that," "I've earned this," or any of a host of other positive frames. Once you have identified one or two positive self-images, you can then take that image or language and apply it to an area where you would like to experience improvement.

It may seem strange, unfamiliar, or downright out of the question given your current circumstances. However, despair not—this is where we begin to integrate principles of choice, visualization, affirmation, and the comfort zone for help.

CHAPTER 11

THE DYNAMICS OF CHOICE

You may not be able to direct the wind,
but you can adjust your sails.

—Variation of a quote by Cora L. V. Hatch, 1859

Before we can explore the dynamics of choice, we first need to back up a bit and re-examine two critical components of choice: *responsibility and accountability*. For most of us, the two words mean pretty much the same thing—who gets the credit or who gets the blame. Responsibility can also mean something about duty, much like a parent is responsible for their child.

Response-Ability

You cannot escape the responsibility of tomorrow by evading it today.

—ABRAHAM LINCOLN

For our purposes, we are going to use *responsible* and *responsibility* in the same way Fritz Perls defined them when he wrote *Gestalt Therapy Verbatim*. As noted earlier, Perls popularized framing *responsible* as *response* and *able* (response-able) and *responsibility* as *response* and *ability* (response-ability) meaning "having the ability to respond."

In this sense, responsibility means that in any given situation, we have a range of possible responses coupled with our ability to implement those responses. Sometimes we have multiple options or responses available to us, sometimes apparently fewer. Of equal importance, we may have greater skill or ability with certain responses or options than with others. Coming up with the best choice for how to proceed then becomes an exercise of determining available options (responses) and weighing those against our current ability or capability.

In some instances, the theoretic "best" response may not be available due to limitations of skill or ability. When that's the case, another set of choices will emerge; should I proceed with a lesser option that is within my current skill set or ability, or am I better off if I first learn the enhanced skill or ability? All kinds of factors enter this equation ranging from timing and urgency to past experience, self-confidence, and what our self-talk may have to say about the situation.

Accountability: Are You Willing to Own the Outcome?

If responsibility means *having the ability to respond,* we then need to consider what it means to be *accountable.* In traditional use, the word derives from French and Latin words meaning to account. Traditionally, accountability means to account for one's actions or outcomes, *after the fact.* In this sense, accountability can easily be construed as fault or blame—"who's accountable (responsible) for this mess?"

For our purposes, however, I am going to propose an entirely different sense of the word. In my coaching and consulting work, I encourage people to reframe accountability as *"the willingness to own the outcome."* With this use, accountability becomes something to assume *before* embarking on a course of action leading toward an intended outcome, rather than something that happens *after* the fact.

If you look back at your Wheel or your Symbols vs. Experience worksheet, you may find areas in which you have a history of "after the fact blame (accountability)"—the self-talk that starts with "I told you that wouldn't work," "just another screw up in a long history of screw ups," "if they had only let me do it my way," or your favorite forms of criticism and blame.

You may also observe areas where you have made great strides. With the benefit of hindsight, you may recognize that before you even began, you assumed the positive version of accountability, often called determination or commitment. "I am committed to this and will do whatever is necessary to achieve my goal (response-ability)."

If you are willing to own the outcome of your desired improvements, then much like Edison in search of the lightbulb or Mitchell looking for ways to overcome his situation, you will keep taking micro-steps, adjusting along the way until you arrive at something workable.

The Downside of Deciding

Whenever you have an opportunity to choose, my suggestion is to make choices, rather than decisions. What's the difference? Not much in the everyday use of language. However, there's a huge energetic distinction between deciding and choosing. Decisions tend to lock us into a prescribed path, while choices keep the door open for new possibilities as we move downstream.

Let's take a moment and deconstruct the words, looking for that energetic distinction.

Starting with *decide*, or de-cide, what other words do you know any that end in "cide?" Do these seem familiar?

- Sui-cide
- Homi-cide
- Patri-cide
- Matri-cide
- Fratri-cide
- Genoc-ide
- Insecti-cide

I'm sure you recognize the pattern. Each of these common words shares the same Latin root word, *decider* (de + caedare) which means to cut, to kill, or to tear apart. Another older meaning is to "stumble accidentally into a snare." In my consulting work, I have often observed people killing off options or possibilities out of ego, stubbornness, or just plain impatience.

If the decision process is one of killing off ideas, few of us want to come up with options only to risk having them killed off or torn apart. Even worse is the possibility that we might wind up stumbling into a snare and being torn apart ourselves.

No wonder people avoid decisions!

However, our critical self-talk may like the process of deciding in the sense that it can find fault with almost any option. "That won't work because," or "that's silly because." You get the idea. Then there are those situations when our self-talk wants us to avoid making any decisions—"I don't care, you decide." Why? Have you ever made a decision only to find someone criticizing you later? "You thought this was a good restaurant/movie/vacation spot?" As much as our self-talk likes to do the criticizing, it doesn't care for outside criticism.

The Upside of Choice

What can you do instead of deciding? Choose! This may seem like splitting hairs, especially since dictionaries typically define choice as deciding and decide as choosing. However, there are major energetic differences.

"Choose" derives from the Latin *gustare* meaning "to taste." Modern definitions include "to have a preference for," "to select freely," and "to take an alternative." Think about visiting an ice cream shop or wine-tasting bar—have you ever asked for a taste before selecting something? If you don't care for the first taste, you can try something else, until you settle on your preference.

This might be the simplest and most effective way to consider choice or the process of choosing. When you ask for the taste, you know you want something, you're just not certain which choice will land you on your desired outcome. If we decide upfront, "chocolate is best because everyone knows vanilla is, well, vanilla," we may wind up eliminating something that we might otherwise enjoy.

Energetically, *choice* implies *a sense of direction or moving toward* something desired whereas *decide* suggests *moving away* (cut out, avoid the snare, kill off).

If you choose toward a desired outcome and it doesn't appear to be working, you are free to choose again (take an alternative).

Decisions made can be hard to redirect, because changing can imply that I was wrong in the first place. I may have argued so strenuously for my decision at the outset that backtracking now is difficult.

Leaning Into

Working on this idea of tasting before committing can also be done inwardly. If you find yourself wanting to create a change of some sort, one way to test the idea is to simply engage your imagination first. We call this inner process, *leaning into* something.

Before settling on a choice or course of action, consult with your soul-talk about the desired outcome, imagine possible choices or next actions, and then *lean into* the idea by imagining taking a step or two in each of the possible directions. You can then "mock up" possible outcomes from the actions you are "leaning into." You may surprise yourself about the perspectives that become increasingly clear in the process. Of course, you may also need to be mindful of the propensity for your self-talk to override even this mental exercise—*Are you nuts? This could never work*—or any of a dozen variations that may be familiar.

In my work, I frequently use the notion of "leaning into" something before jumping in. I recognize that commitment is required to achieve the desired result. However, you can still be fully committed to the outcome without having to be "all in" on the "right" path forward. Instead of "deciding" on the "right path," you can always lean in, "test the waters," "scout the territory," before "betting the house." Notice how many clichés there are for this kind of approach to choosing?

Are You Trying to Solve the Wrong Problem?

No matter how determined you might be to improve your Wheel and your life experience, to make the best choices, you need to be certain that you are focused on solving the right problem.

In the many years I have been working with groups in seminars or teams in organizations as well as with individual clients, I have found that people tend to focus more on the effect of the problem than the actual source. When this occurs, people can become quite adept at "solving" the effect without ever understanding why the problem keeps showing up.

When I was 10 years of age, my family made a trip from the San Francisco Bay Area to Iowa that summer to visit family. One warm evening, we were gathered on the porch, the adults chatting with one another, the kids playing and otherwise waiting for the evening to begin cooling off.

Earlier, my grandmother had draped a blanket over one of the porch rails in case someone needed it if the approaching thunderstorm came our way. As we were playing, I knocked the blanket off the rail, and it fell into the garden dirt below. Uncle George pointed this out and asked me to pick up the blanket and put it back. As I was about to drape the blanket over the rail once again, Uncle George asked if I was going to clean it off first.

I didn't see any dirt because I was looking at the side that was facing up. He pointed out that the dirt was on the other side. So, I turned the blanket over, lay it back on the ground, and cleaned off the dirt. As I was about to put it back, Uncle George again asked if I was going to clean it off. When I protested that I already had cleaned it, he asked me to look at the other side.

I was surprised to see the dirt, so I laid it back down on the ground and cleaned it once again. I'm guessing you can see where this is going—after repeating this process several times, Uncle

George said off-handedly, "I wonder if he will ever learn."

Then it dawned on me that while I was busy cleaning one side of the blanket, I was putting more dirt back on the other side. That's when I figured out that if I draped the blanket over the rail, with the dirt side up, I could both clean the blanket as well as solve the problem of it getting dirty over and over again.

Do you have dirty blankets of your own that you have attempted to clean by focusing on the result without considering the source of the "problem"?

EXERCISE

Consult Your Soul-Talk Before Choosing

You can try this simple exercise in just about any situation requiring a choice or decision on your part. You can do this as a simple meditation or as a written exercise.

Begin by identifying the area under consideration. Invite your true self, your soul-talk to work with you on this area.

- What is the current situation, issue, problem, or opportunity?

- What is your desired outcome?

- What will it look like when you get there?

- What options or choices can you imagine that might be available to you?

- Using your imagination, visualize exercising option A.

  - What might it look like if you exercise that choice? What might it feel like?

- What might be the outcome or outcomes (both the upside potential as well as the downside risk)?

  - Notice any criticism or resistance from your self-talk and write it down.

- Repeat the process with each possible option or choice.

- When you have finished previewing or leaning into each option or choice, consult with your soul-talk for its guidance or recommendation.

- What micro-step can you take to begin leaning into the option or choice?

- Plan to take that first micro-step.

- Schedule a time to review your progress, consulting your soul-talk for additional insights or options.

Blame and Complain Is NOT a Strategy

Shortly after my tear gas experience, a mentor of mine helped me zero in on my self-talk and its proclivity to complain about various aspects of life. Although I had begun awakening to the greater peace, loving, and caring I wanted to experience in the world, I was still caught in my propensity to criticize and complain.

He helped me dig for the underlying message and purpose in my frequent complaints by asking a simple question: *What do you hope to get by complaining?* That one brought me up short, for I had never considered that there might be a purpose or message in my complaining.

My somewhat lame answer had to do with wanting things to

be different and having someone else do something. Even in this simple self-talk response lay a hint from my soul-talk—rather than simply complaining about things as they were, some deeper part of me wanted to become involved in making a difference. I just wasn't ready or willing to risk actual involvement.

He asked me how complaining would make anything different. Of course, I had no good answer. Some part of me equated complaining and criticizing with making real choices as though complaints and criticisms would change anything. Pressing forward, he asked me to consider some choice I could make to transform my complaints into something substantive, something actionable, something I could do to make things better.

One answer was that I could just accept things as they were and there wouldn't be anything to complain about. OK, fine. That could be true. I have learned that acceptance can be a key to experiencing life in greater balance, peace, and equanimity. As we saw in Chapter 3, acceptance is a key requirement before meaningful choices can be even perceived, much less made.

However, as we dug even deeper, he helped me discover a powerful soul-talk message I had from myself, to myself, that was hidden inside the complaint. While my self-talk was busy complaining about how other people seemed to catch more breaks in their lives than I did or how unfair the world was, my soul-talk was underscoring that there were proactive choices I could make that might lead to meaningful differences.

I know, duh! Hidden in my complaints was a kind of demand, a sense of entitlement, that I deserved better, that the world owed me a better set of circumstances. Not only did I want things to be better, but someone else owed it to me. My self-talk was completely sure this was true, reminding me of all the "bad breaks" I had endured from family bankruptcies to living in my car for a time.

My friend and mentor then asked me what I would have to risk to get what I wanted, for the complaints to go away.

That one stopped me cold for a little bit. The more I pondered the question, the more I realized that the way out of my complaints and into a more fulfilling experience involved me doing something about the condition. Whether it was a more fulfilling relationship, a better job, or a better living situation, if anything was going to change, it was going to come down to me doing something about it.

This may seem as obvious as the day is long, but it still didn't quite click sufficiently for my self-talk to receive the inner message and get going. So, we dug some more.

The Hidden Message in Complaints

That's when I discovered a life-changing awareness: *Complaints are signs of something preferred, but not being risked.*

If my self-talk hangs out complaining, I get to keep pretending that not only do I want better, but that I deserve better. And I also get to pretend everything would be so much better, "if only." "If only *they* would just get out of my way and let me run things, boy would things be better around here."

There are several troubling aspects to this kind of thinking and not just the inherent hubris that it takes to hold such a thought. What if I am capable of making things better but just not willing to risk finding out?

What if "they" did let me run things? And what if things didn't get any better? What if things got even worse?

If only was my perfect no-risk scenario—I got to keep telling myself, and anyone who would listen, just how much better things would be *if only* they let me do things my way.

The fly in this ointment is that I wouldn't risk stepping forward to see if I could make the difference I told myself I wanted and was capable of making. So, I continued to live in my perfect fantasy of a better life, letting everyone else know that they're screwing up.

Is there some difference you would like to experience in your life? Jobs? Housing? Health care? The environment?

If you haven't already, I encourage you to begin that thousand-mile journey to create the life you would prefer.

How You Respond to the Issue IS the Issue

Start by doing what's necessary; then do what's possible;
and suddenly you are doing the impossible.

—FRANCIS OF ASSISI

By accepting response-ability for our reactions to anything that is happening around us, we may begin to discover a host of options leading to the improved life experience we truly seek. By recognizing that we are the ones choosing our reactions or responses, the blame and complain game ceases to have power over us. Not that we can't slip back into the game—after all, it may have become all too familiar for so many of us these days. But the game will no longer work as well once we experience that we are the ones choosing how we respond.

Drs. Ron and Mary Hulnick write in their profound book, *Loyalty to Your Soul:* "How you relate to the issue is the issue." Given my focus on response-ability, I am reframing their brilliant phrase to how you RESPOND to the issue, is the issue.

Philosophers have noted this phenomenon seemingly forever. Voltaire quipped, "Every man is guilty of all the good he did not do." That one is worthy of consideration all by itself. Most of us don't have to look too far back in time to identify some choice we avoided, failed to make, or simply deferred to someone else.

Many profess to care about the environment and yet sometimes "step over the trash" in the hallway or on the sidewalk. The choice to step over the trash contributes to the degradation of the environment as well as failing to do the good that was right in front of us. It can be easy to disregard this example as almost inconsequential until we recognize that not much of consequence takes place without those little micro-steps of conscious choice to make small improvements.

"No snowflake in an avalanche ever feels responsible" is another wonderful example capturing this essence. While often attributed to Voltaire, this appears to belong to Polish poet Stanislaw Jerzy Lec, from his 1969 work, *More Unkempt Thoughts*. Regardless of the source, the snowflake metaphor contains a powerful underlying message often echoed in the more common observation: "If you're not part of the solution, you're part of the problem." Stepping over the trash may be just as detrimental to the environment as creating the trash in the first place.

It may be useful to consider the possibility that personal problems avoided, and degrading environments best devolve into one of two questions: "Am I perpetuating problems in my life by my own stepping over the trash" or "Have I forsaken opportunity or good by my own lack of action?"

One of the not-so-obvious-but-oh-so-powerful aspects of this approach to how we experience life is that we don't have to be right with our answers for something useful to emerge. By simply asking the question about our response-ability for good not yet experienced or troubles that have befallen us, we are likely to discover our soul-talk pointing out available choices which could lead to improvement in our current situation.

Self-talk sometimes prefers to stick with the blame and complain game if for no other reason than it's easier to blame someone or something else than it is to accept response-ability and make new choices.

While we may not have a perfect solution, getting involved and taking whatever actions we can begins the process toward improvement. Even a micro-improvement tends to be better than no improvement at all. "Any port in a storm," "Rome wasn't built in a day," and "Perfect is the enemy of the good" are all adages pointing to this simple truth—we need to start somewhere.

By listening more attentively to the encouragement and wisdom of our true self, we can step beyond self-talk–imposed limitations of doubt, blame, complaint, self-criticism, and conflicting beliefs.

Is there some area in your Wheel of Life where you would like to experience improvement? If something is troubling you, if you are beset by challenges, if there is an area where you would like to improve, what could you do about it? What small step can you take to put yourself on the path of improvement?

You might want to take a few moments right here and now to go inside (meditate) and ask what message your soul-talk has for you about your next steps.

EXERCISE

Turning Complaints into Solutions

Pause for a moment right now to think about an area of life where you may find yourself complaining, or perhaps have found yourself complaining in the past. There are a couple of possible approaches to this exercise.

One option would be to write something down about the area of complaint, working with the questions that follow. Another option would be to engage in a simple meditation, asking your soul-talk to explore possibilities with you.

With either option, follow this string and find out where it leads:

- Ask your self-talk: What is it in your life that you find objectionable, unfair, or just not to your liking?

- Imagine: What might it be like if the situation were to change?

- Ask your soul-talk: What small (micro) step could you

take toward that improvement or change? Remember: *directionally correct, not perfectionally correct.*

- Ask your self-talk and soul-talk to align themselves:

    ♦ When could we (our self-talk and soul-talk) take that first step?

    ♦ Will we commit to doing so?

        ○ If so, can we take that first step right now, this very minute?

        ○ If now isn't practical, then put it on your calendar—make an appointment with yourself to take that next micro-step.

- Notice how you feel acting toward your own desired outcome.

- Thank your self-talk for coming along.

Taking even micro-steps can be immensely rewarding.

CHAPTER 12

PAIN IS INEVITABLE, SUFFERING IS OPTIONAL

When we are no longer able to change a situation,
we are challenged to change ourselves.

—Viktor Frankl

What if suffering comes from a lack of acceptance and appropriate response-ability, even in the most dire of circumstances?

Mitchell reminds us that *It's Not What Happens to You, It's What You Do About It.* It would be easy to imagine how he could have allowed himself to indulge in self-pity, complain about how unfair it was, and given up. Had he done so, he would have added an unnecessary element of suffering to the already painful reality he faced. I know I have given up over far lesser circumstances in my own life.

However, as Mitchell understood all too well, had he chosen to focus on blaming others for what had been taken from him, he might have condemned himself to a life of mediocrity at best. Instead, he also understood that he could choose to find opportunity even while dealing with disfiguring burns and paralysis.

If he had chosen the "poor me" approach, his reticular system would have supplied him with an endless "no hope" focus which, in turn, would have led to next to zero choices other than more self-pity.

In the language of Fritz Perls, Mitchell understood his responsibility, his response-ability, for his situation. If he had succumbed to the negative self-talk of responsibility as blame—who's responsible for this "tragedy"—I'm pretty sure he would have found a whole lot of other people willing to agree that someone else was to blame, it was their fault, life is unfair, etc. Their combined agreement would have further doomed him to a life of loss.

By choosing to focus on his response-ability, Mitchell listened more acutely to his true self reminding him that he could make any number of choices about how to respond to his circumstances. Indeed, he chose a proactive response to his situation, albeit with fewer options than before his injuries, but still numerous options, nonetheless. Best-selling author, hall of fame motivational speaker, successful entrepreneur—all possibilities that emerged from the "tragedies" that befell him.

Viktor Frankl—Discovering True Freedom

Viktor Frankl provides another powerful example and reminder about our ability to choose our responses. Frankl was an Austrian psychiatrist taken prisoner by the Nazis along with his wife and parents and transported to the Auschwitz-Birkenau concentration camp. He was soon separated from his family: His wife, Tilly, died in Bergen-Belsen, his father died in Terezin, and his mother and brother were killed in Auschwitz.

In his incredible work, *Man's Search for Meaning*, Frankl writes of his profound experiences in various concentration camps. Under the most horrendous of circumstances, he not only served his fellow prisoners in small but meaningful ways, he also discovered what he later defined as humankind's true source of freedom. Imagine that— learning freedom while in a concentration camp.

Here's a summary of what he learned about freedom from his time in the concentration camps, quoted from *Man's Search for Meaning*:

> *Everything can be taken from a man but one thing: the last of the human freedoms—to choose one's attitude in any given set of circumstances, to choose one's own way.*

Between stimulus and response there is a space. In that space is our power to choose our response. In our response lies our growth and our freedom.

Frankl's powerful response to his experience provides us with incredible insight and guidance we can use for our own life experiences.

(If you find your self-talk telling you these experiences and lessons from Frankl and Mitchell are a bridge too far, you might consider reading *Man's Search for Meaning* (Frankl) or *It's Not What Happens to You, It's What You Do About It* (Mitchell). Both are great sources of amazing life lessons. Perhaps your soul-talk just might be whispering to you, reminding you that the premise of "*What If*" is worth considering.)

If you're willing to play the What If game, your first choice will be how you choose to respond to what happens to you in your life. That initial choice or response is an internal one. If you listen to your negative self-talk, you may find yourself indulging in limitation, obscuring possible choices and ways forward. If you listen more intently to that quieter voice of your soul-talk, you may find, as Viktor Frankl and Mitchell have, that there are forward-moving options available, choices sometimes hiding in plain sight.

I have found that my true self is always pointing me to better options, always encouraging me to find a way forward, a way up, regardless of circumstances. Initially, these micro-steps may not seem like life-changing choices, but they are often the important first steps on that thousand-mile journey to a better life.

Commitment—99% Is a Bitch

If you have an idea of where you would like to improve your life experience and are willing to move past blaming circumstances and other people, then the next important step is commitment.

Lots of people are committed until the going gets a bit rough and their self-talk enters the picture, reminding them that they never really wanted this after all. This begs the question of *what am I committed to in the first place?*

Thinking back to your Wheel and Symbols vs. Experience exercises, the first requirement is clarity about the outcome(s) you are committing to achieving. If the commitment is to the thing or symbol side of the equation, your self-talk just might be correct when it tells you it doesn't matter in the first place. Committing to the symbol or tangible thing may not get what your soul-talk truly desires—the deeper, sustaining experience(s) that outlast anything physical or material.

When we commit to a strategy, project, or course of action without sufficient clarity about the desired outcome (experience), challenges and frustration are sure to arise. Most of us, myself included, have committed to something that no matter how hard we tried, did not work out as we hoped. I have sometimes found myself stubbornly committed to the course of action I chose at some distant fork in the road even when it was clearly not working.

I know there have been countless times when my self-talk has convinced me "that this should work—this time." And so, even in the face of evidence to the contrary, I have kept on trying to push water uphill anyway. This could look like either perseverance or insanity. Perseverance would have me working different approaches while remaining committed to the outcome. Insanity (stubbornness) would have me repeating the same thing over and over again, hoping for a different result.

Edison's lightbulb experience may seem contradictory to this message about the difference between perseverance and insanity. However, his commitment was to the outcome of successfully designing a working lightbulb, not to any particular course of action or combination of gas and filament.

The critical difference begins with clarifying and committing to the desired outcome more than committing to any particular action or pathway. Clarity and commitment to the outcome allow us to choose a different response when the evidence indicates that the current pathway isn't working. It is important to keep in mind that *how we respond to the issue IS the issue.*

Mitchell tells a wonderful story about commitment while in rehab from his paralysis. His therapist was trying to teach him many tasks, which his self-talk labeled "impossible tasks." One of those impossible tasks was learning to transfer from his wheelchair to the couch and back again. But when Beverly, his therapist, initially tried to teach this impossible, even stupid task, his self-talk resisted quite vigorously, arguing why would he need to learn to transfer to a couch? After all, he already had a place to sit. Beverly gave him a good reason.

Beverly asked if he would ever like to share a bit of romance with a woman one day in the future. "Of course," he replied. She then pointed out that before they might wind up in bed together, they would probably start by sitting next to one another on a couch. What was impossible a few minutes earlier, turned into a commitment—in his words, "on the couch, off the couch, on the couch." Transfers were now a reality, well beyond the reach of his self-talk.

The key here, and a very important one that Mitchell emphasizes, is something you will have undoubtedly heard over the course of your life—*99% is a bitch, 100% is a breeze.*

You can watch Mitchell tell this short, delightful, and humorous story on his YouTube channel.

If we are committed to creating the outcomes we truly desire in life, then much like the story of the thousand-mile journey, we won't quit when our self-talk tells us that we have done enough already. The 100% commitment issuing forth from our true self, heard through the quiet voice of our soul-talk, will keep encouraging us to "keep on keeping on," taking as many steps as it takes to complete the journey.

What Are You Pretending to Know?

When looking back at failed efforts, you may be able to identify certain kinds of pretense. Have you ever pretended to have an ability for a response that you did not actually possess? This kind of pretense is so common that it has been catalogued under a couple of different names, two of which come to mind.

The imposter syndrome or imposter phenomenon are psychological terms describing a person who doubts their abilities or accomplishments while experiencing a persistent internalized fear of being exposed as a "fraud." The Peter Principle is a management term coined in 1969 and refers to a tendency in hierarchical organizations for people to rise to their "level of incompetence," for employees to be promoted based on their success in previous jobs until they reach a level at which they are no longer competent. For those who have been promoted past a level of competence, the imposter syndrome may then follow closely.

Do you have any self-talk reminding you that you aren't as skilled or competent as you might like to think (pretend)? If so, you have a couple of creative options. You can take the criticism and run it past your soul-talk for further evaluations and options. For instance, your self-talk may criticize you for not possessing a level of skill which might be true. However, rather than wilt under the internal criticism, your soul-talk might say something like, "Right. We're not as good at that skill as we would like. Now, here's what we can do about it."

The imposter phenomenon and its related issues arise from pretending to know something not yet in evidence. When we act out of pretense, sooner or later the area of pretense becomes increasingly evident, and the pretense catches up with us.

However, as we explored earlier in the Chapter 8 section, "What Are You Seeing That Is Not Yet Visible?" and as we will discover in the next section on "What Are You Pretending Not to Know?" you may perceive a skill, ability, or opportunity not yet in evidence, but valid nonetheless if you choose to accept response-ability for the possibility and take the necessary steps to fulfill the opportunity.

What Are You Pretending Not to Know?

Pretending not to know something can be just as challenging or dangerous as pretending to know. As we noted earlier in Chapter 7, "Intention and Focus: Energy Follows Thought," soul-centered vision can see past what is physically present and into that which is about to become visible. Most of us have been on both sides of this equation where we somehow just "knew it."

Sometimes we can see or sense something and ignore what's being shown. That can be the case of sensing something isn't going to work and plowing ahead anyway. Similarly, we may know or sense something will work and fail to act, ignoring the inner guidance. In the first instance, we wind up creating a "disaster," and in the second, we miss out on a "miracle" or "blessing."

Did You Ever Know It and Blow It?

Perhaps you can recall a time when you chose to embark on a course of action while some part of you was cautioning you to slow down, or not to proceed at all. You may know this one well—something blows up and you immediately recognize that earlier caution—*Damn! I knew it!*

You may have experienced times when you took some action that worked out well, and later said to yourself, or even someone else, *I just knew it would work!* And you did!

A third version of this may also be familiar. Have you ever heard or noticed something that wound up working out, perhaps for someone else, but didn't act on it yourself because your self-talk kept reminding you of some limitation—"don't be ridiculous," or "too good to be true," or "this could never work." And someone else made it work.

You really did see it early on, but your self-talk got in the way of acting on what you saw or sensed inwardly. Once again, you may have lamented to yourself, "I knew it!" This time, with the "Damn" again.

Now, this can be tricky—was the cautionary note coming from your negative self-talk, or a deeper intuition arising from your soul-talk? Learning to differentiate the two is important, which is why there are a few exercises in this book where we invite you to do a form of quieting yourself, meditating if you will, and engage in an inner dialogue between your self-talk and your true self.

We've all "known that" beforehand and denied what we were seeing, allowing it to remain hidden just below the level of conscious awareness. This applies equally to knowing something that will work as well as knowing something that can turn out badly. It can be easy to ignore what we are seeing or hearing inwardly, especially as we are still gaining experience noticing our more subtle inner clues. Again, meditation and consultation with your true self can be extremely helpful in discerning the difference.

Confused, Stubborn, and Determined: Antecedents to Learning

It's easy to become confused about which way to turn. Have you ever found yourself in an argument—with your own self—about which way to go next? The challenge is common, something we all seem to face—one part of us wants to go one way while another thinks quite differently.

As painful as confusion can be, there may be a hidden value in confusion. When you find yourself confused, you may be at a learning point. In my experience, I rarely learn when I'm certain. Why? Because I'm already *certain!*

However, when I'm confused, uncertain, and reduced to the plaintive cry, *I just don't know*, I may be at the doorstep to learning something new—or at least, new to me!

Self-talk can have a way of stepping in and blocking the way to new learning, with inner dialogue ranging from "it's hopeless," to "who cares anyway" to "this is all nonsense." There's something about that inner self-talk that relishes being right, even when it doesn't know.

Do you have a stubborn streak in you somewhere? I know I do. Your self-talk may disagree, insisting that it's just determined, and yet your soul-talk may gently remind you of the difference between being determined and simply being stubborn.

Determination is that aspect of who we are that can help us find a way to reset our sails when the winds change; stubborn is that part that insists on carrying on despite the elements or the apparent reality in front of us.

The word *confuse* itself provides insight into both its meaning as well as its potential value. Merriam-Webster is again helpful:

Confuse:

1: to disturb in mind or purpose: THROW OFF
2a: to make indistinct: BLUR
b: to fail to differentiate from an often similar or
    related other
c: to mix indiscriminately: JUMBLE

The etymology of the word comes from the Anglo-French *confusiun*, borrowed from Latin *confūsiōn-, confūsiō* "mixing, combining, disorder, consternation," from *confud-*, variant stem of *confundere* "to pour together, blend, bring into disorder, destroy, disconcert" + *-tiōn-, -tiō,* suffix of verbal action.

In simple terms, then, whenever we're confused, we need to ask what we may have jumbled together, either out of our own actions and thoughts, or what ideas, thoughts, or beliefs we may have taken on from someone else. It may be helpful to refer to the sections on beliefs in Chapter 10 for examples of conflicting or jumbled thoughts, ideas, or beliefs.

Sometimes, the way forward will require backtracking a bit to unwind the series of conflicting beliefs or information that got us into our current predicament. We may need to challenge our self-talk (beliefs), asking what evidence we have to support the belief or conflicting information.

At other times, we may have done just fine in the past, but now find ourselves stuck in a new set of circumstances requiring new or different approaches. If what we already knew were sufficient, we wouldn't be stuck! Maybe it's time to consider something different, something new, or at least, new to us.

In times of confusion, the loudest voice often wins. However, louder isn't necessarily the same as wiser. Which voice do you listen to more frequently—the softer, quieter voice of wisdom, or the louder, more impatient one? The voice of wisdom, your soul-talk, seeks that which will truly sustain while the impatient, louder voice, your self-talk, often seeks that which will provide a temporary sense of relief or fulfill an immediate desire. Of course, the louder voice never comes right out and tells you that it is going for something illusory or temporary.

Drs. Ron and Mary Hulnick write of this practice in their book, *Loyalty to Your Soul.* In their language, they call choosing the inner voice of wisdom a process of seeing life through "soul-centered eyes." The metaphors are somewhat mixed here, but they work for me in the biblical context of "let him who has ears, hear, and him who has eyes, see."

As you seek an even more fulfilling life experience, ask yourself: To whom are you listening for advice? Are you living life through the eyes and ears of the temporal and ephemeral, or are you looking through the soul-centered eyes of your true self, listening to your soul-talk?

CHAPTER 13

COMFORT ZONE AND CREATING A NEW FAMILIAR

Argue for your limitations and, sure enough, they're yours.

—Richard Bach

While you have undoubtedly heard of and likely encountered the comfort zone at different points in your life, let's consider this question: What does *comfort zone* imply or suggest?

Most people equate the comfort zone with being comfortable, which makes sense on the surface. Being comfortable seems as ordinary as breathing in and breathing out. I don't know anyone who lives life in search of being uncomfortable. However, that doesn't mean there aren't plenty of people who have adapted to discomfort and call it normal, or even comfortable. "I don't want to change. I'm comfortable right where I am, thank you very much."

In my experience, people are most comfortable when things are most familiar. It's a bit like being on automatic pilot. When things are familiar, we don't have to think too much, we don't have to be too much on our toes, we can just go through life picking and choosing our behaviors from an apparently safe, familiar set of choices.

Or are they? Safe, that is?

Do you know anyone who engages in "unsafe" forms of recreation? How about rock climbers? Skydivers? Bungee cord jumpers? The list goes on.

The first time someone tries one of these forms of "entertainment," things are probably a bit unnerving, scary, and surely uncomfortable. However, with enough practice, people can become quite comfortable with something inherently uncomfortable, even dangerous. Why? Because once we become familiar with the process, we know our options and how to perform them. We can even become comfortable doing something physically uncomfortable like ice climbing once we're familiar with it.

Some jobs can can be physically uncomfortable, even dangerous, and yet those doing those jobs can be quite comfortable performing their work. Firefighters are comfortable performing in the face of challenging, uncomfortable, if not downright dangerous situations. Why? Because they have trained for the job and the dangers they are about to face. They know how to behave in the face of extreme heat and danger, and even though the physical situation may be far from "comfortable," they are comfortable nonetheless because they are familiar with the challenges and how to respond.

With enough practice, we can develop the kind of comfort that comes with familiarity for almost any challenging situation. It is the familiar that produces the "feeling" of being comfortable.

How About a Water Landing?

You may recall the story of Chesley Burnett "Sully" Sullenberger, the USAir pilot who "landed" his Airbus A320 on the Hudson River in 2009 with 155 souls on board despite losing all power after striking a flock of geese. It would be a real stretch to say Sully was "comfortable" in the usual sense of the word. Yet his familiarity with flying and emergency procedures allowed him to stay calm, even "comfortable," while safely bringing the plane to the river.

None of his training involved landing a plane on a river without power, at least not a real plane in real flight in real danger. However, his training in flight simulators gave him enough "experience" responding to emergency scenarios that when the real emergency arrived, he was familiar with his choices.

One way of thinking about this kind of "heroic" response is that his self-talk was quieted by the preparation he had already done in the flight simulator. Perhaps his soul-talk was there to remind him that he was prepared even though the situation was highly stressful and far from "comfortable."

How does this apply to me, you might ask? While you may not have a physical flight simulator for those changes you would like to experience in your Wheel of Life, you do have some tools that can help. And you already use them, perhaps not in the most useful ways, but you do use them.

I'm talking about what you allow yourself to think about, what you focus on in your mind. We referred to this earlier in Chapter 7 in "The Neuroscience of Focus" section. The more we entertain a thought or pattern of thoughts, the more familiar they become. The more familiar they become, the more comfortable we become.

Remember, *energy follows thought*. If your negative self-talk keeps reminding you that you never succeed in saving money, losing weight, or getting what you want, you may find yourself in the process of creating a very limiting, even negative, comfort zone. That may seem odd—how can a person become comfortable losing all the time?

All the mental "rehearsals" of failure create a comfort zone of familiarity with coming up short. You may know how to fail, lose, come up short, and how to keep on anyway. However, you may not be as familiar with what it's like to win, succeed, or improve. If this sounds familiar, then you may find yourself "trying" to get better only to have your self-talk keep reminding you, "hey, we tried this exercise stuff before —it never works out. In fact, all we ever get is tired."

There are whole books dedicated to the fear of failure, while others suggest that it's the fear of success that gets in the way. The general argument goes something like this: Given how many times you have failed in life, how could you be afraid? You already know how to fail and survive! However, success is a different matter—what would happen if you succeeded? Would people expect more from you? Would you expect more from yourself?

Negative self-talk causes the brain to produce cortisol, which is a kind of internal signal that danger lurks. As you consider straying outside the boundaries of your comfort zone, the negative self-talk triggers more negative thoughts which in turn help the brain release more cortisol, all to save you from yourself, from another dose of danger or failure.

Have you ever imagined taking on something new only to have your negative self-talk warn you against even trying? As your self-talk reminds you of past failures or points out possible dangers, it reinforces familiar patterns of holding back. Those internal repetitions of negative outcomes establish the comfort zone even more deeply while simultaneously programming your reticular activating system to be on the lookout for snares and pitfalls. And, sure enough, with that kind of negative focus, you will find plenty of evidence of possible danger and reasons not to proceed.

Think of this process as engaging your internal flight simulator only in a negative way, practicing coming up short repeatedly. If you continuously crash and burn in your imagination, why would you ever take a risk in real life, be it something new or something ordinary?

However, you can put that internal flight simulator to use in a positive, supportive manner. Just like Sully in the airplane flight simulator, anything you imagine repeatedly is a form of mental rehearsal or practice, which serves to build a platform for a new "familiar."

Practicing the kinds of affirmation and visualizations discussed earlier allows your imagination to begin laying new tracks in your brain. (It's called neuroplasticity.) Those new tracks can build new comfort zones. With enough practice, you can develop the willingness and confidence to engage in new behaviors, leading to improvements or successes in your Wheel not previously experienced.

Create Your Own Internal Flight Simulator

Here's a simple exercise you can try to see what develops. It will take a bit of focus (remember, we go where we focus) and commitment, but if you give this a shot, you may well experience some meaningful results. (This builds on the "Maintaining a Positive Focus" story from my Mind Dynamics experience I shared with you in Chapter 9.)

1. Pick an area where you would like to experience improvement (let's use beginning a regular exercise routine as an example).

2. Every morning *before you get out of bed*, spend two minutes imagining (visualizing) how good you would feel by exercising (even just a couple of minutes—no need to see yourself in a two-hour gym circuit—just a small step to get started).

   a. What might other people say to you as they notice your exercise commitment and how good that would feel?

   b. See yourself celebrating your exercise and feeling good about yourself.

   c. Imagine telling yourself something good about what you did.

3. Every evening as you lie in bed *just before you go to sleep*, spend two minutes repeating the same visualization process from the morning. Imagine how good you would feel by exercising.

a. What might other people say to you as they notice your exercise commitment and how good that would feel?

b. See yourself celebrating your exercise and feeling good about yourself.

c. Imagine telling yourself something good about what you did.

4. If you want a little extra boost, try this same mental exercise sometime around midday.

Adding a simple positive statement to repeat to yourself as you practice these two-minute visualizations can prove to be quite helpful as well. Something as simple as, "I love the healthy, vital way I feel exercising every day" can be very effective. And here's a real kicker, *do not exercise unless you REALLY feel like it.* This little tip is to remind yourself that you are not laying another guilt trip on yourself—you only exercise when you feel like you really want to, *not because you should.*

Notice that all we're asking you to do here is "practice" feeling good twice a day in your internal flight simulator for a total of four minutes (or three times and six minutes if you go the "extra" mile).

This process produces a new kind of familiarity, that of loving the healthy way you feel from exercising, which then crosses over into feeling great about physically exercising. The more you practice these little two-minute "flight simulator" drills, the more familiar (comfortable) you will become with the notion of exercise. With repetition, you may find that you become uncomfortable if you don't exercise. The sense of familiarity and comfort that builds over time from these little internal practice sessions can spill over into your life pattern and become your "new normal."

You can apply this same kind of two-minute practice to anything on your Wheel, or any area of life for that matter. The sidebar on the next page has a personal example from my own life, a bit corny perhaps, but real, nonetheless.

CREATING A NEW NORMAL

Back in the early 1980s, David Allen and I were crafting a program to help people accomplish more in life, something we wound up calling the MAP Seminar—Managing Accelerated Productivity. Today, you may know that program as *GTD —Getting Things Done.*

As part of the training program, we encouraged people to imagine changes they wanted to experience in their businesses.

In addition to visualizing the improved future so the reticular formation could get on board, we also encouraged people to create affirmations for the change.

David helped me learn a new-to-me key for making affirmations work when he had me create an affirmation around flossing my teeth. I know this may seem a bit prosaic to say the least, and yet it served as a great lesson for me. You might find it beneficial as well.

My dentist at the time had a wonderful poster in his office, something your self-talk may relate to: *There's no need to floss all your teeth, only the ones you want to keep.* I don't know about you, but I felt guilty because "I knew better," and yet just couldn't bring myself to floss every day as "I knew I should."

David suggested an affirmation focused on how I would like to experience myself from flossing (remember the earlier work on Symbols vs. Experience). I imagined what it would feel like and then came up with this corny affirmation: *I love the healthy way my mouth and gums feel from flossing every day.*

A bit dumb, my self-talk told me.

David, however, provided this bit of advice, which I followed diligently: *Do not ever floss your teeth because you think you should; only floss if you really, really feel like you want to.*

A month or so went by, and I repeated the affirmation a few times each day (I had it taped on my bathroom mirror so I would see it at least twice each day). One day, I was leading a seminar at the Miramar Hotel in Santa Monica when we came to the part of the program where we addressed the role of the reticular formation in creating successful outcomes from goals and projects.

I introduced the piece about affirmations and gave the example of flossing my teeth that I was currently working on. As I said the affirmation out loud the first time to that class, I noticed an uncomfortable feeling in my mouth. I repeated the affirmation and became even more uncomfortable. I felt so uncomfortable in my mouth, it was as though I had boulders stuck between my teeth. Giving everyone a few minutes to begin writing out their ideal scenes and affirmations, I made a mad dash to the hotel gift shop where I was able to buy some dental floss. As I flossed my teeth, I had the delightful experience of "loving the healthy way my mouth and gums felt."

To this day, I not only floss every day, but I keep dental floss in my desk drawer, next to my reading chair, in the living room, in my briefcase, in my car, in the bathroom—and I probably am leaving out a few locations—because *I love the healthy way my mouth and gums feel from flossing every day.*

Completion: Your Laters Are Already Here

Most of us have a collection of half-read books, partially accomplished goals, and so-so experiences in life. The more things remain incomplete, the more they have a way of dragging us down, blocking our ability to move forward. When we tell ourselves we are going to do something, there's a part of the brain that holds onto that commitment and keeps reminding us that it still needs doing, draining energy and focus we could use in other areas. Conversely, whenever we complete even simple commitments, we release mental energy which we can use to create more of what we truly prefer in life. (You can read more about this by Googling the Zeigarnik effect.)

One of the major roadblocks to completion centers around timing and when we will take the action necessary to bring about the changes we truly desire. One downside of the comfort zone and power of the familiar is that we may have learned over time that we can pretend we're going to move on this, just sometime in the future—later.

As David and I were developing the MAP seminar, we learned a great deal from Dean Acheson, a great mentor who shares a name with President Truman's secretary of state. He taught us some key principles around creating focus and clarity. One of those principles was around Next Actions—micro-steps that get us going—coupled with the idea that not everything we think about needs action now but might be useful to track for later—something Dean called "Someday."

We landed on the term, "Someday, Maybe" as a way to help people distinguish between the actions they were committed to taking and those "good ideas" they might want to consider for another day, "Someday." We suggested that people create a Someday, Maybe list for actions that they *might* want to take someday but did not have any current commitment to implement.

Someday, Maybe lists help keep track of those good ideas without adding the burden of implied commitment—"Did I really mean it? If so, then why aren't I doing something about it, NOW?" Commitment minus action often leads to guilt and eventually erodes self-confidence—*sure I'm going to move on this idea, just like all the other good ideas I said I would do "later."*

However, for some of us, "Someday, Maybe" can be dangerously close to *I'll do this LATER.* The distinction, which may seem minuscule, centers around the notion that I may want to move forward in an area and keep telling myself that I will do it "later," a kind of deferred commitment. Someday, Maybe simply indicates "maybe," but without the commitment implied by "later."

When our self-talk is hesitant about moving forward out of any number of reasons (self-doubt, the comfort zone, conflicting intentions, or simply the concern that something could go wrong), "later" seems like a safe way out. Our self-talk can keep telling us that we will do it later, "pretending" that we will move on it when we get *around to it, LATER.* (This issue is so universal there's even an old joke about people needing to find "a round tuit" to help get things done. These days, you can find hundreds of "round tuits" for sale on the Internet.)

The problem with "later" is that later may never seem to come, or as my spiritual teacher used to say over and over again, "you're in your 'laters' now."

(If you want to take a deeper dive into completion and the power of next actions, you might want to read David Allen's best-seller, *Getting Things Done: The Art of Stress-Free Productivity.*)

Your Seemingly Impossible Good: Creating Your Ideal Scene

Life can be pulled by goals just as surely as it can be pushed by drives.

—VICTOR FRANKL, *MAN'S SEARCH FOR MEANING*

Now that we know *there's only one energy,* that *energy follows thought,* and *the universe rewards action, not thought,* let's turn our attention to using that energy to produce great results, to create the life of your dreams.

My wife, Dr. Inez Bishop, helps people create *Ideal Scenes,* a way of thinking about and energizing what they would like to create or experience in their lives. She typically has people start with two phrases that work like caveats.

The first phrase is a bit of protection: *this or something better for the highest good of all concerned.* That's a way of letting the universe and our internal sources of energy know that we only want the ideal scene to come true if it's in alignment with our highest good. This simple phrase acts as a set of guardrails to protect against wanting something, getting it, and then wondering why you ever wanted it in the first place. In a very real, but subtle way, *this or something better for the highest good of all concerned* is an affirmation coming directly from the true self.

The second phrase, *my seemingly impossible good is happening now,* is equally important. This phrase reminds us internally that possibility exists beyond anything we may have experienced so far. If you blend how the reticular formation works in conjunction with *energy follows thought,* you may get a sense of how this works.

Together, both phrases become affirmations of what we intend to create and help align the energies of our self- and soul-talk in service to our desired outcome. It is also important to note that *my seemingly impossible good is happening now* is framed in the present tense. It is not some wishful dream for the future, which never seems to arrive. If we were to say, *my seemingly impossible good will happen soon* (or anything future-focused), "soon" never seems to arrive. "Soon" is always just a day away.

By framing your Ideal Scene in the present tense, you may discover that your self- and soul-talk begin to align as the reticular formation finds evidence of choices available *now* that can help move in the desired direction. By taking those micro-steps *now,* the object of your focus starts to take shape, *now.*

The more you review your Ideal Scenes, the more likely you are to discover and take the steps necessary to get you there. Keeping in mind "micro-steps" and the thousand-mile journey, you don't need to take giant strides or even the "right" next step to bring about your *seemingly impossible good*. Much like driving a car or riding a bike, it's much easier to steer once you get the process moving.

One of those micro-steps could be practicing the morning and evening visualizations described earlier—in your internal flight simulator.

If you are interested in experiencing this kind of Ideal Scene work, Inez does not charge for these sessions; instead, she views it as a service, a way of giving back. If you would like to arrange an Ideal Scene session with her, please visit my website (www.russellbishop. com) and use the contact form to let me know of your interest. I will help make this happen.

CHAPTER 14

OVERCOMING YOUR OWN RESISTANCE

What you resist, persists.

—Carl Jung

As you will recall from Chapter 3, "Acceptance," it's pretty much impossible to make progress or changes without first acknowledging and accepting the reality of the current situation. However, our self-talk may throw up various forms of resistance.

Resistance can be obvious when it shows up as plain old stubbornness. Some of the more familiar versions of stubborn resistance are *no, I'm not going to . . .* or *. . . you can't make me . . .* or the ever-popular, *don't confuse me with the facts, my mind is made up.*

Stubbornness is typically born out of a fear of being shown up or proven to be wrong about something. The more energy we have invested "proving" or insisting that our solution is right while other options are just plain wrong, the more likely we are to become resistant to alternative approaches.

Resistance can be a form of denial when we don't understand something or fear we won't be able to find our way forward. You're probably familiar with a common form of self-talk denial: "*this can't be happening.*" Of course, most of the time when this one shows up, we have recognized the situation, and "*this can't be happening*" is simply a form of negative acceptance. Self-talk may add more color commentary, perhaps along the lines of: "*Wouldn't you know it—bad things always happen to me.*" Or "*How could they/it/this.*"

In certain circumstances, this simpler form of resistance melts into begrudging acceptance. Have you been there? I'll bet something like this scenario is familiar—the tire goes flat, "*this can't be happening*," followed by a lot of muttering, cursing, or other negative self-talk directed either at yourself (should have known this would happen sooner or later) or directed to someone else (who paved this road anyway, cheap tire manufacturer, etc.).

Cursing the flat tire or ranting about who's at fault are examples of what I call adding negativity to an already negative situation. In addition to adding negativity to the situation, begrudging acceptance can also result in resignation, a form of negative acceptance that leads to what I earlier described as "settling for less." It's a form of giving up, because "Well, what's the use? I'm stuck. There's nothing I can do."

It's easily understandable to describe the flat tire as a negative situation. However, much like with Mitchell, once we move past the data point of flat tire, severe burns, paralysis, etc., there's not much to be gained by cursing the situation, lamenting our bad luck, or blaming the universe. Begrudging acceptance, negative focus, and negative self-talk will not help change the tire, heal, or learn new ways of moving any faster. Instead, they may well slow you down or even prevent your recovery.

Pain Is the Price You Pay for Resisting Life

You may have heard this refrain coined by Carl Jung—*what you resist, persists*. As long as I'm busy fighting the flat tire, the injury, or whatever, the condition continues to persist, lessening the likelihood that I will find anything useful to help. The situation might even worsen. If I'm busy cursing the flat tire, I may wind up with scraped knuckles trying to change the tire (which I have done). The situation is already negative enough without having to add even more negativity to it.

Or, as I like to say, *pain is the price I pay for resisting life*. Pain could be physical (scraped knuckles), emotional, or mental. Or even all three.

Stress is a mental and emotional pain response that presents physically when my mind (self-talk) keeps telling me something isn't fair or right or should be different. Whenever I persist in holding any kind of negative thought, my emotions will likely rise to match the thought (remember, *energy follows thought*). I can then wind up with an upset stomach, headache, high blood pressure, or any of a dozen other manifestations of "stress."

Judgment

Judgment is a common form of resistance that most humans know all too well, a human trait that masquerades as being right or self-righteousness. Our self-talk seems predisposed to believing that it is right.

Have you experienced a flat tire, an injury of some kind, or simply been displeased about how someone else is living their life? If so, rather than simply recognizing and accepting what's so, your self-talk may have jumped into the fray, not only blaming someone else for the circumstance (which might even be true in the case of the laundry van that crashed into Mitchell) but adding negativity to the situation in the form of mental/emotional pain by judging the person or event as inherently bad, wrong, or otherwise deficient.

One of the problems with judgment is that when we judge, it can often seem to placate some part of the situation, a kind of misapplied sense of soothing, as though the act of judging somehow made the situation better or more palatable. Of course, if we want to move on from the negative situation, judging won't help—it only prolongs the "suffering" until we finally choose to do something about it. Again, as Mitchell reminds us, at the end of the day, *it's not what happens to us, it's what we choose to do about it.*

My self-talk often reacts to situations I don't like by getting angry, upset, or agitated as though that would somehow make a difference. Not surprisingly, upset, judgment, and blame rarely produce a change for the better. In my experience, judgment usually makes the desired change or relief that much more difficult to bring about and often adds even more negativity (stress) to the experience.

Are You Drinking Your Own Poison?

Have you ever been so upset with another person or what they did, that you not only judged what they did but also carried resentment toward them? Have you ever held onto that resentment even when they weren't present? If so, you may recognize a sinister aspect to judgment—resentment often accompanies judgment.

A quote that has been attributed to everyone from Saint Augustine to Nelson Mandela to actress Carrie Fisher seems to underscore the challenge here: "Resentment is like drinking poison and waiting for the other person to die." A somewhat different metaphor works as well: "resentment is like picking up a hot coal to throw at someone else without realizing it's your hand that will get burned." It's as though our self-talk may be convinced that we are punishing the other person by holding onto resentment.

Even if our self-talk is "right" in judging what the other person did, we may be poisoning ourselves all the while thinking we are somehow punishing the other person by remaining upset.

The Power of Forgiveness—the Way Out

If you find you and your self-talk stuck in judgment, resentment, or the blame game, there is a way forward. Forgiveness.

Most people think of forgiveness as something we offer to another person or group. That kind of forgiveness can be wonderful, healing even. Nelson Mandela could be one of the most iconic representations of the power of forgiveness. After decades of imprisonment for the color of his skin in South Africa, he wrote and said repeatedly, "Forgiveness liberates the soul, it removes fear. That's why it's such a powerful weapon."

Judging another also carries a hidden burden, something your soul-talk knows all too well. When judging another, we forget (fall asleep to the fact) that the other person is also a soul. As soon as we judge another, we unconsciously judge the soul, the Divine, within them. By judging the Divine in someone else, we also separate ourselves from that same Divinity, and therefore from our own soul.

Abraham Lincoln put it this way: "I don't like that man. I must get to know him better." He also said: "Am I not destroying my enemies when I make friends of them?"

If you find that your self-talk can be critical (judgmental) of others, I'll wager that you are also critical (judgmental) of yourself. Just as judging another person separates me from recognizing the Divine in the other, judging myself separates me from recognizing the Divine within my true self. The pain we feel in judgment or criticism is the pain we experience in our own separation.

When we experience the pain of separation, it is quite common to add even more pain to the situation by heaping on even more judgments. It might go something like this: "Jeez, this is even worse than I thought. How could they be so (mean, stupid, nasty, etc.)." There's also the personal version—*what's wrong with me, how could I be so (fill in the blank)*. And now we have a self-talk, self-reinforcing downward spiral. The more I remind myself just how bad this is, the more negative emotions I seem to feel—negativity begetting more negativity. In this case, negative energy follows negative thought.

The more you work with the quieter aspect of your true self, the more you may discover that your soul-talk has a natural inclination toward compassion, empathy, and forgiveness. For some of us, it is easier to be compassionate, empathetic, or forgiving with others than it is to be compassionate and forgiving of ourselves. Forgiving yourself for judging yourself is a very gentle yet powerful process that can be of enormous value in liberating yourself from the pain of separation.

Meditation on Forgiveness

If you find yourself in judgment, regardless of whether it is directed toward someone else or yourself, take a moment to quiet yourself, perhaps starting with a breathing meditation. As you invite your soul-talk to be more present, you can practice a different form of forgiveness—self-forgiveness.

You can use this simple exercise just about anywhere, and it only takes a minute or two. However, simply reading this meditation is very different from participating in the exercise, much like reading the prescription label is different from taking the medicine.

Once you have quieted yourself and invited the presence of your true self, bring to mind the person or situation you are judging or toward whom you are feeling resentful. Start by allowing your soul-talk to say these words to yourself (to your self-talk):

> I forgive myself for judging (person) for (whatever they did).

> I forgive myself for judging myself for feeling (negative feeling).

> I forgive myself for forgetting that they are Divine.

> I forgive myself for forgetting that I am Divine.

You might also consider applying this forgiveness meditation to any situation in your life that you would like to improve. Are you judging anything about your life? Your job or your boss? A key personal relationship? Your health?

Try this one out a few times and you may discover a whole new level of freedom inside yourself. At the very least, you may find that this process is the antidote to the poison called resentment.

CHAPTER 15

THE POWER OF A POSITIVE FOCUS

Listen to your Soul before you give credence to your mind.

—John-Roger, DSS

As you continue to free yourself from the negative bonds of resistance and the limitations of your self-talk, you will probably find that you need your soul-talk to help you hold a more positive focus as you move forward.

Rarely does internal guidance show up as lightning and thunder or some other form of the dramatic. It seldom provides a detailed roadmap either. Instead, it tends to reveal itself in the quiet of your soul-talk. By practicing the meditations throughout this book or your preferred form of inviting the presence of your true self, you may find that you can develop an increasing ability to see that which is not yet visible, to hear the inner guidance.

By holding a positive focus, you can begin tapping into a deeper power or ability to create the life you want rather than the one you may have settled for. However, there's a huge gap between daydreaming about a better life and doing the work necessary to turn your dreams into reality.

From my own life experiences, I know all too well the challenges of holding a positive focus in life, whether from experiencing family bankruptcies while growing up, being homeless for a time, losing precious relationships, or having business opportunities melt during tough economic times. Along the way, I have learned that simply holding a positive focus is an invaluable key to overcoming adversity. However, simple is not the same as easy.

Positive Thinking Alone Doesn't Work

As we discussed in Chapter 7, positive thinking alone won't work; it takes positive action to produce a positive result. By acknowledging what's present, moving into acceptance, and letting go of resistance, denial, or judgment, you may discover positive choices that can help bring about the changes you would like to experience.

Nowhere along the line did Mitchell ever pretend that being badly burned and paralyzed was something wonderful. However, he did move from acceptance into a positive focus on what he could do about his circumstances.

Of course, you don't have to be dealing with something as dire as paralysis for these lessons to apply. You could be doing just fine in your life and still be open to things going even better. Your life can be going just fine and still have room for improvement.

If you would like circumstances to change for the better, you might ask yourself when you would like to start? So often I hear people say they will get around to it "later." If that seems familiar, remember that your "laters" are already upon you. Don't let your self-talk pretend that you will do something different, "later," without a commitment to doing the work. If you're not sure, you can always use your Someday, Maybe list to track it so you can make a choice one way or the other down the road.

It's All About Those Micro-Steps

As you practice holding a positive focus, you may only come up with a couple of micro-steps at first, and micro-steps clearly won't take you from zero to hero in one sudden leap. Micro-steps just get you moving, and it's a lot easier to steer once you are moving. Starting with a positive focus on an improved experience of life can lead you to those first important micro-steps.

As you begin moving, remember to keep acknowledging yourself for your progress, that you are on your way, and that things are in the process of becoming just a little bit better. From there, your reticular system will likely begin filtering in more opportunities, more choices, and more micro-steps that you can consider taking. The more opportunities and choices you perceive, the more your mindset will begin to shift from bad and getting worse to good and getting better. The more you make that inner shift, the more you will find your self-talk and soul-talk coming into greater alignment. As you continue making real-world choices that begin adding up to a real difference, you may even find your self-talk becoming more positive.

EXERCISE

Creating Positive Change or Improvement

You may find it helpful to pull out your Wheel of Life again. This time pick an area where you would like to experience improvement over the next few months.

As you settle in on that one area, follow these simple steps and observe what takes place inwardly.

1. Identify the area of desired change or improvement.

2. Close your eyes for a few moments and simply imagine how you would experience your life as this area improves:

   a. Imagine feeling better and better about the area, about yourself, about your whole experience of living. What feelings do you imagine sensing?

   b. Imagine seeing specific changes and how you will look as these changes take place. If others would see or notice the difference as well, what might they see as you progress through these changes? What kinds of looks on their faces can you imagine?

c. Imagine what you will hear as these changes take place. How might you hear your self-talk changing? What might you hear others saying about the positive differences they are noticing or experiencing with you?

3. As the visualization becomes increasingly clear, create a short, positive affirmation of the changes as if the changes have already having taken place. Here are some starter thoughts to get you going:

a. I love the healthy, vibrant, and energetic way I feel as I take care of my body, health, and well-being.

b. I am having great fun and enjoyment as I____

c. I am experiencing grace and ease as I____

d. Every day, in every way, I am getting better, better, and better.

e. I am earning a great income doing what fulfills me.

f. I have perfect work for perfect pay.

g. I am appreciating who I am and the many blessings that surround me.

4. Practice the visualization and affirmation for two to three minutes each morning as soon as you awaken and again for two to three minutes as you lie in bed just before you fall asleep.

a. Feel free to return to the visualizations and affirmations during the day if you like.

b. Write your affirmation and place it where you will see it during the day—perhaps on your bathroom mirror or on a blank business card you can place with your wallet or keys.

c. And remember *never* do anything until you *really* feel like moving on it.

Transform or Transcend?

You can't have a physical transformation until you have a spiritual transformation.

—CORY BOOKER

Traditionally, the process of personal change has been called *transformation*. In many ways, this whole book is about transforming your life. In my experience, *Becoming More of Who You Truly Are* involves transformation as well as a step up from transformation.

As I have come to learn, *transformation* can be the first major shift on the path toward something even more significant. When it takes place, it can feel as though whole new worlds have opened. Digging a bit deeper, you may discover as I have that there are several subtle distinctions in the process of transformation that can be lost on your self-talk but ever so appreciated by your true self. Bear with me and notice what you notice.

TRANSFORMATION means to create *a change in form or appearance*, implying a *major change in form, nature, or function*. In working with thousands of people all around the world, I have noticed that some people will settle for minor changes, hoping for a major transformation. There may well be some areas of life where a simple change will be sufficient, perhaps even significant.

However, there's a potentially hidden limitation in the process of transformation. In one sense, transformation can be likened to owning a Volkswagen and wanting an upgrade. One form of upgrade might entail buying a fancy car kit, say something like a Ferrari, and putting the fancy car body over the Volkswagen frame and engine. It sure looks different, yet underneath, it's still a Volkswagen. Nothing wrong with VWs to be sure—I used to own one and loved it! However, if you're looking for a Ferrari-like change, and you settle for a Ferrari lookalike, disappointment may be just around the next curve.

Oher metaphors apply, including one you may have heard before: "That's like putting lipstick on a pig." Nothing wrong with pigs, mind you. Lipstick just won't change anything.

If you discover that a change in form or appearance isn't getting you where you want, you may be looking to transmute something about your life experience. *TRANSMUTATION* implies *transforming something to a higher element or FREQUENCY, to something for the better*. This is where your soul-talk comes into greater focus.

While your self-talk may have you focusing on VW-to-Ferrari type changes, your true self would likely prefer moving into a higher frequency, transforming not only the physical nature of a *thing* (Symbols vs. Experience) but also the qualitative or energetic experience along the way. If we apply the notion of *there's only one energy*, it could be that the kind of change your true self seeks is a change in frequency or energy more than a change in the symbolic side of things.

Ultimately, you may find that your soul-talk is encouraging you to *transcend* your current situation for something remarkably different. Merriam-Webster tells us that to transcend something means:

- "to rise above or go beyond the limits of"

- "to triumph over the negative or restrictive aspects of "

- "to be . . . *beyond and above* the universe or material existence."

Indeed, you may discover your true self communicating an internal yearning to live beyond the apparent limitations of the material world, calling you to *lead a soul-centered life*, by *Becoming More of Who You Truly Are.*

And here's the not-so-secret hiding in plain sight: *You already know where your true self would have you go, what your true self would prefer to experience.* All you have to do is listen to its messenger, to your soul-talk. As Rumi and St. Francis noted centuries ago, *becoming more of who you truly are* means you already are the one you seek to become.

As you continue moving through the various stages and changes in your life, you may experience something calling you into a greater depth and possibility, something beyond what you may have settled for along the way. You may have already experienced that inner calling. It will be no surprise that the "something" is your soul-talk, your true self, calling you forward.

Nothing I have written here is intended to convince you of something, to change your beliefs, to alter your life goals. What I have shared here are observations from 50+ years of working on myself while assisting thousands of others to do the same.

If you were to simply believe what I have written without putting it to the test, you will have missed the whole point. If, however, you were to apply some of these exercises, some form of quieting your self-talk and inviting your soul-talk to take the lead, you may be stunned by the wisdom, guidance, and love that come forward, opening the doorway to a life so rich, fulfilling, and uplifting that all you will be able to do is live in gratitude.

CHAPTER 16

THE GRATITUDE CONCLUSION

*Wear gratitude like a cloak, and it will feed
every corner of your life.*

—Rumi

Gratitude could be one of the most important skills we can learn and practice daily. Ultimately, how we experience life comes down to a fundamentally simple choice: where we choose to place our focus. In my experience, gratitude is the most powerful, enduring, and uplifting focus we could choose.

My life has been filled with so many simple yet powerful blessings that I have often lost sight of them in the apparent complexities of my day-to-day life. The more I have learned to develop an attitude of gratitude, the more I have discovered that no matter what may have befallen me over the years, including the difficult times of living in my car with only six dollars to my name, who I truly am has always been just fine—not necessarily the "I" of my personality, ego, or self-talk, but the deeper aspects of who I truly am, my true self. Only in retrospect has it become clear to me that regardless of how circumstances have changed over time, who I truly am has always been just fine, neither better in one set of conditions nor worse off in others.

My true self, my soul, is always just fine. Always has been, still is, always will be. I have learned that all I need to experience that all is fine is to notice where I place my attention. I am fond of reminding myself that "peace is present; the only question, am I present with the peace." Even in challenging situations, when I remind myself to look inwardly, past my self-talk, I can usually find that my true self remains absolutely fine.

When we allow our negative self-talk to take the lead with its litany of criticisms, cautionary notes, and glass-half-empty perspectives, we are guaranteed to find evidence of our negative focus. As we saw in Chapter 7, the reticular formation will find evidence to support our focus. If instead, we allow our true self to lead, our soul-talk will lead us to positive, uplifting experiences, even in the face of seemingly negative circumstances. As Mitchell reminds us, "Before I was paralyzed there were 10,000 things I could do. Now there are 9,000. I can either dwell on the 1,000 I've lost or focus on the 9,000 I have left."

No one would have faulted him for lamenting his situation, and yet he chose to turn the apparent negative into a positive—not a positive set of circumstances, but positive life experiences. His choice to focus on the 9,000 left is a perfect example of an *attitude of gratitude.* The more he focused on what he had, the more he found the ability to build a positive, fulfilling life.

The Science of Gratitude

The Greater Good Science Center at UC Berkeley has found that developing an attitude of gratitude can produce lasting neurological changes affecting how we learn and make decisions. Other positive benefits from expressing gratitude include improved emotional and mental health states. At the simplest level, people who choose to focus on gratitude tend to be happier. (You can read more on their research online.)

Research at the HeartMath Institute in Boulder Creek, California, shows that practicing gratitude can produce positive changes in heart rate variability and lowering stress levels. In an article published in the National Institutes of Health's National Library of Medicine, HeartMath researchers report that a simple practice of appreciation and gratitude can lead to a reduction in cortisol levels and a corresponding increase in DHEA/DHEAS. (You can read the abstract online.)

Practicing gratitude, even for just a few minutes, begins to reset the focus held by our reticular formation. If we let our true self lead, we can create a life that is good and getting better. Keeping in mind that *energy follows thought*, it takes no more effort to appreciate the good we have in our lives than it does to dwell on what's missing. The more we focus on gratitude, the more we seem to have to be grateful for.

Most of us have gifts and blessings all around us and rarely seem to notice. My wish is that you will be able to apply some part of what has been written here, enabling you not only to notice those gifts and blessings, but also to build on them, to create a life of meaning, fulfillment, and great satisfaction.

EXERCISES

Develop Your Attitude of Gratitude

If you would like to experience deeper levels of satisfaction in your life, it could be as simple as developing a greater appreciation for what you already have. There are several simple practices or exercises you might consider experimenting with.

- *Gratitude Journal:* Write something each day for which you are grateful. This could be a practice you use as the day comes to an end. What positive experience did you have this day? It doesn't have to be earthshaking to be relevant—it could be something as simple as appreciating a meal, a smile, time with a pet, or a sunrise or sunset. By writing notes about what you appreciate, no matter how small, you will begin to program your reticular system to notice even more positive occurrences. That, in turn, may lead to discovering previously unnoticed opportunities to experience even greater good in your life.

- *Gratitude Letter:* Think of someone who has been helpful to you sometime in your life and write them a letter. It could be someone from your past as well as someone in your present. What do you appreciate about them? What are you grateful for? You might choose to send this letter, or as the Greater Good folks tell us, the benefit develops inwardly even if you don't send the letter. It's all about expressing gratitude.

- *Gratitude Meditation:* Start with your breathing and focus on your heart. Recall a time you felt grateful inside and do your best to re-experience that feeling. You might remember a time you visited a special place, or the love you feel for a friend, or even for a pet you love. Allow those positive feelings of appreciation and gratitude to linger and notice how you feel as you do. You might imagine extending those positive feelings into the day ahead, filling the day to come with the warmth of your gratitude and appreciation. Given how the reticular system works, you may then begin to notice even more opportunities to be grateful as you go through the day. The hidden value of this exercise is that no matter how the day unfolds, you will already have experienced those positive feelings.

- *Gratitude Affirmations:* Affirmations can be helpful in reprogramming your focus as you go through each day. As you create gratitude affirmations, remember that they need to be positive in focus, moving toward your desired outcome and framed in the present tense. They reinforce your desired outcomes and help keep your creative process focused.

Here's a starter set to get you going. Please edit these to make them personal and meaningful to you.

1. I experience gratitude, joy, and peace in every day.

2. I am grateful for who I am.

3. I am grateful for the life I'm living.

4. I am grateful for the blessings in my life, both big and small.

5. I am grateful for my family and friends.

6. I am grateful to have shelter and food.

7. I am grateful for the beauty of nature.

8. I am grateful for the little things in life.

9. I am grateful to be alive.

More Gratitude and Acknowledgments

Normally, acknowledgments come at the beginning of a book. In this instance, I feel compelled to conclude with an overview of gratitude for those who have helped me grow, develop, and discover more of who I truly am. The risk here is that I will undoubtedly leave out many who have contributed to my well-being, some whom I may have never noticed, others whom I am simply overlooking.

Here goes:

- My loving wife, Dr. Inez Bishop, who loves and supports me beyond my limitations, who truly sees the good and the God in everyone.

- Ernie Gourdine, who held me on those trying days at UC Davis and awakened me to the source of my inner strength behind my apparent fear and fragility.

- Fritz Perls for the gift of awareness.

- Albert Einstein for demonstrating the interconnectedness of all things, showing that physics, metaphysics, and spirit are all part of the human experience.

- Carol Star for introducing me to John-Roger.

- My sisters, Janice and Sally Bishop, who have shared in this life story and demonstrated their own forms of compassion, resilience, and love.

- My mom, who kept me focused on what is possible and contributed to some profound yet simple lessons, not the least of which was "Can't died in the poor house because he couldn't."

- My dad, who demonstrated the ability to keep doing his best regardless of circumstances.

- John-Roger, who showed me the power of the inner worlds through meditation and *spiritual exercises*. There are so many other lessons I could call out, I could write an entire book just on those lessons, so I'll leave it to being my Way Shower, helping me awaken to my true self, to my soul.

- John R. O'Neil, who provided years of patient guidance, support, and encouragement without ever crossing the line into telling me what to do.

- David Allen, who partnered with me in so many ways: learning, teaching, sharing, growing, loving, accepting, understanding, forgiving—well, the list goes on.

- John Morton, who consistently steps forward, following divine guidance, and demonstrating the courage to take the next step even when the stair isn't visible.

- Frances Hesselbein, who awakened me to the power of seeing that which is not yet visible.

- Ben Cannon, who reminded me that nothing is surprising if I simply notice without fear of judgment.

- Tim and Jinny Ditzler, for their many years of support, encouragement, love, and reminders that each year can be my Best Year Yet.

- Marshall Goldsmith, whose simple question, "how can I help you have a better life" serves as a profound guiding light of service, acceptance, and awakening.

- Bruce Fetzer, for his courage to carry forward a legacy of answering the Call from Spirit.

- Bob Roth, for helping countless thousands awaken to the transcendent power of meditation.

- Valerie Bishop, who continues to lovingly encourage and support me in making this work available.

- Dr. Marc Darrow, who counseled me at a time when I was struggling through self-doubt, with these powerful words: "Your gifts were not given to be lost in your unworthiness."

- Jsu Garcia, who consistently demonstrates great loving and courage sharing love, light, grace, and peace with thousands around the world.

- Eric Hoffer, who helped me learn that I can never get enough of what I don't really want.

- Leigh Taylor-Young, for her steadfast commitment to sharing loving, grace, peace, and joy with everyone, everywhere.

- Arianna Huffington, for helping bring Insight to the UK and her unwavering commitment to awakening the planet.

- The brothers Joe Hubbard, Michael Hubbard, and David Raynr, for showing me the courage of awakened teenagers and carrying this work even farther into the world.

- Pauli Sanderson, who continues to serve in profound ways, helping thousands awaken to the inner light and who never seeks the spotlight herself.

- Candace and Stu Semigran, who steadfastly serve the greater awakening no matter the apparent hurdles or obstacles.

- Sam Westmacott, a delightful being who has been a loving supporter and beacon of light for thousands in the UK.

- Raz and Liza Ingrasci, for your commitment to bringing love in the world and for the gift of the Hoffman Process which has served so many in the path of awakening.

- Ron and Mary Hulnick, who pioneered spiritual psychology, the ability to see through soul-centered eyes and the commitment of *Loyalty to Your Soul.*

- Paul Kaye, Vincent Dupont, and Mark Lurie, who demonstrate a life-long commitment to making spiritual teachings available.

- Leslie Boyer, Mary Ann Somerville, Peter Felsmann, Tom Boyer, and the entire Insight team of facilitators.

- Gary Krebs and his amazing team of editors, who took what I thought was a decent draft and made it even better.

And so, I am wishing you will open your heart to all these blessings and let them flow through you. That everyone you will meet on this day will be blessed by you, just by your eyes, by your smile, by your touch, just by your presence. Let the gratefulness overflow into blessing all around you. Then it will REALLY be a good day.

—BROTHER DAVID STEINDL-RAST

APPENDIX: EXERCISES AND RESOURCES

Box Breathing

Breathing practices can be very helpful in preparing your inner environment for doing the deeper work necessary to listen to and work with your true self, to hear your soul-talk. If you have a breathing practice that already works for you, please do go with what works. If you are not accustomed to doing breathwork, you may find box breathing is a good place to start.

Box breathing is a simple technique that a person can do anywhere, including at a work desk or in a café. Also known as square or 4x4 breathing, this technique is taught in all manner of environments from MDs specializing in stress management to Navy SEALs and yoga studios. It can help you shift your energy and connect more deeply with your body, decreasing stress and introducing a state of calm or restfulness. You can use this technique just about any time, anywhere.

Before starting, sit with your back supported in a comfortable chair and your feet on the floor.

1. Close your eyes and breathe in through your nose while counting to four slowly. Notice the air entering your lungs.

2. Now gently hold your breath inside while counting slowly to four. Try not to clamp your mouth or nose shut. Simply avoid inhaling or exhaling for another count of four.

3. Next, slowly, and gently exhale for another count of four.

4. At the bottom of the fourth count, pause and hold for a count of four.

5. Repeat steps one to four at least three times. Ideally, repeat them for four minutes, or until you feel deeply relaxed or calm.

Meditation: Working with Your True Self

Invite your true self to come forward (feel free to substitute your inner master if you prefer, or your soul).

- Some find it helpful to imagine they are in a peaceful place in nature, undisturbed by the day-to-day world. Others prefer to focus on their heart. There's no wrong way to do this, so just let yourself find your own relaxing, safe space and follow your own rhythm.

- Remaining in this quiet state, consciously invite that deeper part of you, your true self, to come forward as though it were sitting or standing in front of you. At first, you may not notice much difference, at least not in your body, mind, or emotions. You may simply feel more peaceful. Some will notice a presence, and some will even "see" a more defined form, perhaps even an image of yourself.

- As you begin to get a sense of this inward presence, tell it about an area you would like to work with, an area for greater clarity or sense of direction.

- Begin by reviewing the area of concern and any thoughts you already have on the subject. Literally "speak" to your true self as though it were physically in the room with you right now. Let your true self know what you have been thinking including any limiting, critical aspect of your self-talk. Ask your true self or soul-talk what it would prefer that you notice or focus upon. You might want to ask your true self for its recommendations about a different choice you could consider making about what you want out of your life right now.

- Feel free to make this more like a conversation with a trusted friend—pretty much a free-form exchange. Your soul-talk may have questions for you, ideas to consider, or suggestions for new options. Sometimes, your true self will be direct with its advice or preferences. Rarely will the tone be harsh; rather, it most likely will be loving, supporting, and nurturing.

- If you hear something that you don't quite understand, be sure to ask for clarification.

- Repeat what you are hearing and how you imagine it can be implemented. Then ask if you heard correctly.

- Once you and your true self feel complete, thank your true self for its support and guidance, and return to your breathing process.

- When you are ready, slowly allow your eyes to open and focus back into the room where you find yourself.

- Write down what you heard.

What Do You Want?

For these questions to produce real meaning, you may need to cycle through them over and over a few times to allow deeper levels of awareness to filter up, asking more deeply each time "and why would that matter to me?"

- You can ask these questions as a mental process, or perhaps more powerfully as a focus for your next meditation.

- You might also consider keeping a journal or notebook as you return to these questions, writing answers to the questions posed as well as tracking any insights that you discover.

- Reviewing notes, answers, and insights can often lead to a more powerful awareness as you discover connections not previously perceived.

What do you want?
What experience are you hoping to find?
What difference would that make to you?
Why does that matter to you?
What do you want?
How could you get it?

The Wheel of Life

The Wheel of Life is a way to graphically examine the level of satisfaction you are experiencing in your life on several dimensions.

- *Roles you play in life.* Examples might include spouse, parent, manager, colleague, team member, coach, team leader, friend, family member, or breadwinner.

- *Areas of life important to you.* Examples might include artistic or creative expression, positive attitude, personal growth, spiritual growth, career, education, family, friends, financial freedom, physical challenge, pleasure, or public service.

- *Combination of roles and important areas.* Feel free to make this very personal, reflecting priorities or areas of interest.

Feel free to re-label any of the dimensions. I have simply taken the liberty of providing some of the more common ones I find in my coaching work.

To work with the Wheel, look at each dimension as though the center of the wheel represented zero and the outer edge of each "spoke" represented 100 in terms of how satisfied you are with each area.

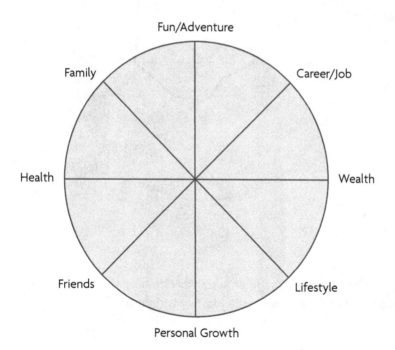

The first step is to place a dot on the line somewhere between zero (the center) and 100 (the outer edge of the circle) for each of the eight elements or spokes. For example, if you were completely satisfied with your health, then you would place the dot at the edge of the circle; if you were only 50% satisfied, then you would place the dot on the Health line about halfway between the center of the circle and the outer edge. Do that for each of the eight elements.

Once you get all eight dots in place, go ahead and connect them. You might wind up with something that looks like this:

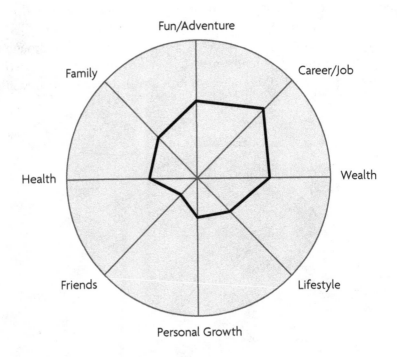

How does the shape of your wheel reflect your current experience of life, how smooth the journey is right now?

- What does the wheel suggest about where you place your focus compared to the outcome or experience you most desire?

- How much time and energy are you placing in the various areas?

- What is the relationship between focus and time spent working on an area and how much satisfaction do you experience?

- Is there an area where you would like to experience greater satisfaction?

- What micro-step can you take now that will begin moving you toward your desired outcome?

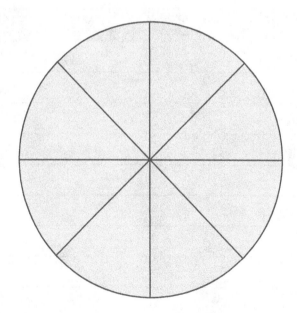

Symbols vs. Experience

Consider completing the left-hand column of the table which follows for each spoke of your wheel. I have labeled the left-hand column "Symbols" to represent the tangible things people often focus on in their life pursuits. "If only I had (a certain amount of) money." Or the right house, new car, better job, etc. For some people, even relationships can be relegated to the level of "thing" or Symbol— think of those people who strive for the perfect "trophy" relationship—not for the quality of the relationship, but for advantages they hope will follow.

The point here is to delineate as truthfully as you can, that which you find yourself focusing on in life, those *things* you want or want more of. These *things* go in the left-hand column.

SYMBOLS	EXPERIENCE
Money or Wealth	
House	
Health	
Toys (golf clubs, boats, etc.)	
Travel	
Perfect Relationship	
Job	
Career	
Etc.	

In the example on page 196, money is one answer to the question "What do you want?" Spend a little time reflecting on the question, "Why do I want those things?" "What do I hope will be true if I have the (job, money, house, etc.)?" Your self-talk may start with something easy and obvious, perhaps something like this: *I want more money because then I could buy more things, take better vacations, etc.*

If you look more deeply inside, how would your soul-talk answer this question: "What positive *experience* or experiences would you associate with having more money?"

Let your soul-talk provide the answers and then place those *experiences* that you are seeking in the right-hand column. It might look something like this:

Turning Complaints into Solutions

Pause for a moment right now to think about an area of life where you may find yourself complaining, or perhaps have found yourself complaining in the past. There are a couple of possible approaches to this exercise.

One option would be to write something down about the area of complaint, working with the questions that follow. Another option would be to engage in a simple meditation process, asking your soul-talk to explore possibilities with you.

With either option, follow this question string and find out where it leads:

- Ask your self-talk: What is it that you find objectionable, unfair, or just not to your liking?

- Imagine: What might it be like if the situation were to change?

SYMBOLS	EXPERIENCE
Money or Wealth	Freedom
Health	Security
House	Fun
Car	Excitement
Toys (golf clubs, boats, etc.)	Happiness
Travel	Love
Perfect Relationship	Peace of Mind
Job	Success
Career	

SYMBOLS	EXPERIENCE

- Ask your soul-talk: What small (micro) step could you take toward that improvement or change? Remember: *directionally correct, not perfectionally correct.*

- Self-talk and soul-talk alignment:

  - When could you take that step?

  - Will you?

    - If so, how about taking that step right now?

    - If now isn't practical, then put it on your calendar—make an appointment with yourself to take that next micro-step.

- Notice how you feel about taking action toward your own desired outcome.

- Thank your self-talk for coming along.

Forgiveness Meditation

If you find yourself in judgment, regardless of whether it is directed toward someone else or yourself, take a moment to quiet yourself, perhaps starting with Box Breathing. As you invite your soul-talk to be more present, you can practice a different form of forgiveness—self-forgiveness.

You can practice this simple exercise just about anywhere, and it only takes a minute or two. However, simply reading this meditation is very different from actually participating in the exercise, much like reading the prescription label is different from taking the medicine.

- What is your self-talk judging or criticizing about yourself or your life?

- What is your self-talk judging or criticizing about others
  in your life?

Once you have quieted yourself and invited the presence of your
true self, bring to mind the person or situation you are judging or
toward whom you are feeling resentful. Start by allowing your soul-
talk to say these words to yourself (to your self-talk):

> I forgive myself for judging (person) for (whatever they
> did).
> I forgive myself for judging myself for feeling (negative
> feeling).
> I forgive myself for forgetting that they are Divine.
> I forgive myself for forgetting that I am Divine.

You might also consider applying this forgiveness meditation to
other situations in your life that you would like to improve. Are you
judging anything about your life? Your job or your boss? A key personal relationship? Your health?

- What is your soul-talk encouraging you to explore or
  accept?

- What difference might that make if you were to listen
  more closely?

Try this one out a few times and you may discover a whole new
level of freedom inside yourself.

Transforming Self-Talk to Soul-Talk

Start by describing a goal for some aspect of your Wheel that could stand improving. It could be anything from changing careers to building up your savings or improving your health.

Once you have a goal in mind, then create a two-column chart of different messages self-talk and soul-talk might have for you.

SELF-TALK	SOUL-TALK
You're never going to make this work.	I'm creative and I can find a way.
Why bother? People like us never succeed.	I can always improve.
You idiot!	I'm a good person who makes mistakes.
The road ahead is just too difficult.	I only need to take one step at a time.
Are you kidding? You have no idea how to do this.	Of course I can—I just need to learn a bit more.

Consult Your Soul-Talk Before Choosing

You can apply this exercise to just about any situation requiring a choice or decision on your part. You can do this as a meditation or as a written exercise.

Begin by identifying the area under consideration. Invite your true self, your soul-talk, to work with you on this area.

- What is your desired outcome?

- What will it look like when you get there?

- What options or choices can you imagine that might be available to you?

- Using your imagination, visualize exercising option A.

  - What might it look like if you exercise that choice? What might it feel like?

  - What might be the outcome or outcomes (both the upside potential as well as the downside risk)?

  - Notice any criticism or resistance from your self-talk and write it down.

- Repeat the process with each possible option or choice.

- When you have finished previewing or leaning into each option or choice, consult with your soul-talk for its guidance or recommendation.

- What micro-step can you take to begin leaning into the option or choice?

- Plan to take that first micro-step.

- Schedule a time to review your progress, consulting your soul-talk for additional insights or options.

Micro-Steps, Visualization, and Affirmations for Making Changes in Your Wheel of Life

You may find it helpful to pull out your Wheel of Life again. This time pick one area where you would like to experience improvement over the next few months.

As you settle in on that one area, follow these simple steps and observe what takes place inwardly.

1. Identify the area of desired change or improvement.

2. Close your eyes for a few moments and simply imagine how you would be experiencing your life as this area improves.

3. Imagine feeling better and better about the area, about yourself, about your whole experience of living. What feelings do you imagine sensing?

4. Imagine seeing specific changes and how you will look as these changes take place. If others would see or notice the difference as well, what might they see as you progress through these changes? What kinds of looks on their faces can you imagine?

5. Imagine what you will hear as these changes take place. How might you hear your self-talk change? What might you hear others saying about the positive differences they are noticing or experiencing with you?

6. As the visualization becomes increasingly clear, create a short, positive affirmation of the changes as if the changes have already taken place. Here are some starter thoughts to get you going:

a. I love the healthy, vibrant, and energetic way I feel as I take care of my body, health, and well-being.

b. I am having great fun and enjoyment as I____

c. I am experiencing grace and ease as I____

d. Every day, in every way, I am getting better, better, and better.

e. I am earning a great income doing what satisfies me.

f. I am appreciating who I am and the many blessings that surround me.

g. Practice the visualization and affirmation for two to three minutes each morning as soon as you awaken and again for two to three minutes as you lie in bed just before you fall asleep.

h. Feel free to return to the visualizations and affirmations during the day if you like.

i. Write your affirmation and place it where you will see it during the day—perhaps on your bathroom mirror or on a blank business card you can place with your wallet or keys.

j. And remember *never* do anything until you *really* feel like moving on it.

Other Resources

Experiential Programs:

- Insight Seminars

    ◆ The core themes of Insight Seminars focus on awareness, responsibility, accountability, and choice. Insight continues to offer programs as a nonprofit educational organization operating all over the world. Well over one million people have participated in Insight Seminars in the US, Great Britain, Europe, Israel, Russia, Africa, Australia, and South America, discovering more of who they truly are and finding ways to integrate that expression of the true self into their daily lives. You can learn more about Insight at www.insightseminars.org.

- Movement of Spiritual Inner Awareness

    ◆ MSIA teaches the principle of Soul Transcendence, focusing on becoming aware of yourself, your true self, as a soul, and as one with God. The soul is who we truly are, more than the body, thoughts, or feelings.

- University of Santa Monica

    ◆ USM offers soul-centered experiential learning empowering students to convert everyday life experiences into rungs on the ladder of their spiritual awakening.

Books:

- *Forgiveness: The Key to the Kingdom* by John-Roger

- *It's Not What Happens to You, It's What You Do About It* by W. Mitchell

- *Man's Search for Meaning* by Viktor Frankl

- *Getting Things Done* by David Allen

- *Workarounds That Work* by Russell Bishop

ABOUT THE AUTHOR

Russell Bishop, the creator of Insight seminars and a recognized expert in personal and organization transformation, has helped thousands of individuals around the world create balance and success in their personal and professional lives. He is the managing partner of Conscious Living, where he coaches people and organizations on how to establish meaningful change aligned with their true purposes in life. His seminars, coaching, and consulting sessions provide a new approach to integrating the experience of wellbeing with high levels of productivity. Over two million people have benefited from programs designed by Russell. In addition to running his consulting practice, he served as Editorial Director for the Living section of the *Huffington Post* and authored *Workarounds that Work*. He resides in Santa Barbara, CA.